THE CHURCH
and
THE LAW OF NULLITY OF MARRIAGE

7113

THE CHURCH
and
THE LAW OF NULLITY
OF MARRIAGE

The Report of a Commission
appointed by the Archbishops of Canterbury and York
in 1949
at the request of the Convocations

LONDON

S·P·C·K

1955

First published in 1955 by
S · P · C · K
Northumberland Avenue, London, W.C.2
Made and printed in Great Britain by
William Clowes and Sons, Limited, London and Beccles

MEMBERSHIP OF THE COMMISSION

The Right Reverend and Right Honourable J. W. C. WAND, D.D., Lord Bishop of London (*Chairman*).

The Right Reverend W. M. ASKWITH, D.D., Lord Bishop of Gloucester.

The Right Reverend C. M. CHAVASSE, O.B.E., M.C., D.D., Lord Bishop of Rochester.

The Right Reverend N. H. CLARKE, M.A., Lord Bishop of Plymouth.

The Reverend E. W. KEMP, B.D., Lecturer in Canon Law in the University of Oxford, Fellow and Chaplain of Exeter College, Oxford, Canon of Lincoln.

The Right Reverend K. E. KIRK, D.D., Lord Bishop of Oxford.[1]

The Reverend L. L. KNIGHTALL, M.A., Rector and Rural Dean of Stanhope, Co. Durham, Honorary Canon of Durham.

The Reverend F. E. P. S. LANGTON, M.A., Vicar of St Mary the Virgin, Bourne Street, S.W.1.

WILLIAM LATEY, Esq., M.B.E., Q.C.

NOEL MIDDLETON, Esq., Q.C.

H. J. PHILLIMORE, Esq., O.B.E., Q.C.

The Reverend A. S. PICTON, M.A., Vicar of St George's, Preston, Canon of Blackburn.

The Reverend E. C. RATCLIFF, M.A., Ely Professor of Divinity in the University of Cambridge, Fellow of St John's College, Cambridge, and Canon Residentiary of Ely.

J. E. S. SIMON, Esq., Q.C., M.P.

The Reverend R. A. TALBOT, M.C., B.D., Vicar of Knaresborough, Yorks.

The Right Reverend H. A. WILSON, D.D., Lord Bishop of Chelmsford.[2]

The Reverend A. F. SMETHURST, Ph.D., Synodical Secretary of the Convocation of Canterbury, Chancellor and Canon Residentiary of Salisbury Cathedral (*Secretary*).

[1] Died in 1954. He had signed the Report.
[2] Resigned 1950 on resigning his See.

v

INTRODUCTION

1. *Terms of Reference*

IN APPOINTING the Commission your Graces stated the terms of reference as follows:

To examine the laws of Nullity, ecclesiastical and civil, and questions relating thereto, in their general and practical bearings.

The Archbishop of Canterbury also sent a letter to the Chairman, in which he stated that the Commission would have to examine Civil and Ecclesiastical Law; judge the Church's position in relation thereto; and consider how the Church should deal with specific cases as they arise, and whether, in certain cases where a decree of Divorce had been granted and the Church satisfied itself that a plea of Nullity could have been sustained on proper grounds, the Church should in such cases allow remarriage in Church as if the decree had been one of Nullity.

2. *Matters referred to the Commission by the Convocations*

Two specific questions arising out of the present revision of the Canons Ecclesiastical of 1603/4, now being undertaken by the Convocations of Canterbury and York, have been referred to this Commission:

(*a*) Canon XXXVI, Clause 2, as proposed by the Canon Law Commission. This Clause reads as follows:

If in regard to a marriage which has been duly dissolved by secular law the Bishop of a diocese, sitting with his Chancellor, is satisfied that there were good grounds upon which such marriage could, instead of being dissolved, have been declared to be null and void, it shall be lawful for such Bishop in his discretion to allow either of the parties to such marriage, although the other of them is still living, to marry, or to be married to, another person, according to the rites and ceremonies of the Church of England, in like manner as if such first mentioned marriage had been declared to be null and void.

When this Clause was debated in the Upper House of Canterbury Convocation it was agreed that the question of the inclusion of some such Clause should be referred to this Commission.

In the course of the debate on this matter the Archbishop stated:

The Commission on Nullity will obviously have to consider the whole of this proposal. Whether or not the Church should make this kind of provision will be the main thing with which the Commission will have to deal. It will not, however, be the only subject which will be before them. They have also to consider whether, for instance, there are any respects in which we are dissatisfied with the Nullity laws of the State, and whether, on any point, they conflict with our laws.

Further than that, I hope this Commission will investigate the administration of the laws of Nullity of the State itself, which, in several recent cases, has got into difficulties in deciding what Nullity really is. My own hope is that the Commission will go deeply into the question of what, in the light of recent cases, is to be regarded as Nullity.

I would suggest that whatever may be done about this proposal now before us, it cannot conceivably be done within the framework of Canon XXXVI. It seems to me that that goes without question. This clause 2 is quite obviously not adequate to the situation. . . . I also hope that whatever is done will be put in a Canon by itself, headed "Of Nullity", and not in a sub-division of something else. I should think that if this Commission wants a Canon it will be a pretty long and elaborate Canon. This is not our only opportunity of making a Canon. If we want to come back and insert a Canon on it, we can do so."[1]

(b) An additional Clause proposed to the draft Canon XXXVIII. This Clause would read as follows:

No person whose marriage has been declared null and void by secular authority under Section 7 (1) a of the Matrimonial Clauses Act, 1937,[2] shall be married in Church to a second partner, so long as the partner to the marriage then declared null and void is still living.[3]

When the Canon was discussed, it was agreed by the Upper House of Canterbury Convocation that the proposed Clause should be referred to the Commission.

3. Subject and Scheme of the Report

There are cases in which a union reputed or purporting to be a marriage is defective in some essential element. Such a marriage is said to be void or

---

[1] The whole discussion of this question as reported in the *Canterbury Chronicle of Convocation* for January 1950 and the *York Journal of Convocation* for May 1949 is worthy of attention.

[2] Now Section 8 (1) (a) of the Matrimonial Causes Act, 1950, which reads as follows: "that the marriage has not been consummated owing to the wilful refusal of the respondent to consummate the marriage." See Appendix 1, p. 49 below.

[3] See *Chronicle of Convocation*, January 1950, p. 95.

voidable, and the defect may be declared and the marriage annulled by a decree of Nullity. This decree must be clearly distinguished from a decree of Divorce, which affirms that the marriage in question was in all respects a valid one, but that it is now being terminated.

The wording of a decree of Nullity is as follows:

The Marriage is pronounced and declared to be and to have been to all intents and purposes null and void in the law whatsoever.

We divide our consideration of this subject of nullity into the following chapters:

Chapter VI CHURCH AND STATE:

> General considerations—Conclusions on the present Civil Law of Nullity (Proposed rejection of *wilful* refusal to consummate as a ground of nullity; Suggested acceptance by the Church of England of other new grounds introduced in the Act of 1937; Possible doubts about epilepsy as a ground; Application of the doctrine of Approbation urged where a child has been born; Consideration of homosexuality as a ground of nullity)—Suggested reforms of the Canon Law—New Ecclesiastical Courts or machinery for relaxing Church discipline in cases of alleged Nullity negatived—Judgements of Civil Courts to be recognized, but legal profession to be invited to co-operate in bringing about judgements of Nullity instead of Divorce in appropriate cases—Discussion of proposed amendment to draft Canon XXXVIII—Suggested new Canon on Nullity of Marriage

Chapter VII CONCLUSIONS AND RECOMMENDATIONS

There follow a number of appendices.

4. *Acknowledgements*

In investigating the matters submitted to it, the Commission has held twenty-five meetings, including a three-day Residential Conference at Oxford.

The Commission has received valuable help from the undermentioned who have submitted memoranda, and some of whom were personally interviewed:

The Reverend D. Sherwin Bailey, PH.D., Lecturer, Church of England Moral Welfare Council.

E. A. Bennet, Esq., M.C., M.A., Sc.D., M.D., D.P.M., Physician, Bethlem Royal Hospital and the Maudsley Hospital, Lecturer, London University Institute of Psychiatry, Senior Psychiatrist, West End Hospital for Nervous Diseases, London.

The Reverend G. B. Bentley, M.A., who was responsible for moving in the Convocation of Canterbury in May 1949 the request that the Commission be appointed.

The Reverend R. G. Heard, M.A., M.B.E., M.C., University Lecturer in Divinity, Cambridge, and Fellow of Peterhouse.[1]

---

[1] The Commission learned with deep regret of the death of the Rev. R. G. Heard in 1952.

The Reverend Professor E. O. James, D.Litt., Professor of the History and Philosophy of Religion in the University of London.

The Reverend G. D. Kilpatrick, D.D., Dean Ireland's Professor of Exegesis in the University of Oxford.

A. T. Macmillan, Esq., Barrister-at-Law.

The Right Reverend R. C. Mortimer, D.D., Lord Bishop of Exeter.

The Reverend Gilbert Russell, M.B., Ch.B., Psychiatrist, Education Secretary, Church of England Moral Welfare Council, 1945–1950, Vice-President of the National Marriage Guidance Council.

H. C. Squires, Esq., C.M.G., D.M., F.R.C.P., D.P.H., Medical Inspector in Nullity to the High Court of Justice.

CONTENTS

CHAPTER I

THE NATURE OF MARRIAGE IN CHRISTIAN DOCTRINE

1. *Introductory*

THE OBJECTS of marriage are stated in the Book of Common Prayer[1] of 1662 as follows:

First, It was ordained for the procreation of children, to be brought up in the fear and nurture of the Lord, and to the praise of his holy name.

Secondly, It was ordained for a remedy against sin, and to avoid fornication; that such persons as have not the gift of continency might marry, and keep themselves undefiled members of Christ's body.

Thirdly, It was ordained for the mutual society, help, and comfort, that the one ought to have of the other, both in prosperity and adversity.

These objects were re-stated in the following terms by the Convocations in the proposed Prayer Book of 1928[1]:

First, It was ordained for the increase of mankind according to the will of God, and that children might be brought up in the fear and nurture of the Lord, and to the praise of his holy name.

Secondly, It was ordained in order that the natural instincts and affections, implanted by God, should be hallowed and directed aright; that those who are called of God to this holy estate, should continue therein in pureness of living.

Thirdly, It was ordained for the mutual society, help, and comfort, that the one ought to have of the other, both in prosperity and adversity.

The very existence of society as we know it is bound up with the institution of marriage. It has taken many different forms; but there are strong anthropological and biological grounds for the belief that monogamy is the normal form of marriage among human beings. In a memorandum submitted to this Commission, Professor E. O. James[2] summarizes the evidence on this matter and states: "The form of *marriage* that has been universally adopted and generally approved has been monogamy, because it alone meets

[1] In the Exhortation at the beginning of the Form of Solemnization of Matrimony.
[2] Appendix 9, p. 70 below.

the fundamental requirements of human personality and of society rooted in the family."

2. *New Testament Teaching on the Permanence of Marriage*

As our terms of reference are limited to the subject of nullity, we do not propose to embark upon a discussion of the full New Testament teaching about marriage, but rather to confine ourselves here to a consideration of certain points which bear directly upon our inquiry.[1] The principal of these is the permanence of marriage. In this connection we consider first the evidence of the Gospels and then of the Epistles. In the Gospels the following passages require consideration:

It was said also, Whosoever shall put away his wife, let him give her a writing of divorcement: but I say unto you, that every one that putteth away his wife, saving for the cause of fornication, maketh her an adulteress: and whosoever shall marry her when she is put away committeth adultery.

(Matt. 5. 31–2.)

And there came unto him Pharisees, tempting him, and saying, Is it lawful for a man to put away his wife for every cause?

And he answered and said, Have ye not read, that he which made them from the beginning made them male and female, and said, For this cause shall a man leave his father and mother, and shall cleave to his wife; and the twain shall become one flesh? So that they are no more twain, but one flesh. What therefore God hath joined together, let not man put asunder.

They say unto him, Why then did Moses command to give a bill of divorcement, and to put her away?

He saith unto them, Moses for your hardness of heart suffered you to put away your wives: but from the beginning it hath not been so.

And I say unto you, Whosoever shall put away his wife, except for fornication, and shall marry another, committeth adultery: and he that marrieth her when she is put away committeth adultery.

(Matt. 19. 3–9.)

And there came unto him Pharisees, and asked him, Is it lawful for a man to put away his wife? tempting him. And he answered and said unto them, What did Moses command you?

And they said, Moses suffered to write a bill of divorcement, and to put her away.

But Jesus said unto them, For your hardness of heart he wrote you this commandment.

[1] For a more general discussion of the subject, see the report of the Joint Committees of the Convocations, *The Church and Marriage*, S.P.C.K., 1935.

But from the beginning of the creation, Male and female made he them. For this cause shall a man leave his father and mother, and shall cleave to his wife ; and the twain shall become one flesh: so that they are no more twain, but one flesh.

What therefore God hath joined together, let not man put asunder.

And in the house the disciples asked him again of this matter.

And he saith unto them, Whosoever shall put away his wife, and marry another, committeth adultery against her: and if she herself shall put away her husband, and marry another, she committeth adultery.

(Mark 10. 2–12.)

The law and the prophets were until John: from that time the gospel of the kingdom of God is preached, and every man entereth violently into it.

But it is easier for heaven and earth to pass away, than for one tittle of the law to fall.

Every one that putteth away his wife, and marrieth another, committeth adultery: and he that marrieth one that is put away from a husband committeth adultery. (Luke 16. 16–18.[1])

It is generally agreed that Mark's is the earliest form of these sayings. With his clear teaching that marriage is to be regarded as indissoluble except by death, Luke agrees. Matthew, however, inserts a permission to the husband to break the bond if the wife is guilty of *porneia*, a term that in our official versions is translated "fornication." This would seem to imply a departure from the straightforward principle enunciated in St Mark's Gospel. It is to be noted that the question put to our Lord is not the same in the two Gospels. In Mark's version he is asked: "Is it lawful for a man to put away his wife?", which is the equivalent of saying "Is divorce permissible?"; whereas in Matthew's version the question is: "Is it lawful for a man to put away his wife for every cause?", i.e., "In what circumstances is divorce permissible?" This seems to link the Matthean version with a first-century Jewish controversy between the schools of two Rabbis. The dispute originated in varied interpretations of the Mosaic command referred to in Matt. 5. 31; 19. 7; and Mark 10. 4. That command is to be found in Deut. 24. 1–2:

When a man taketh a wife, and marrieth her, then it shall be, if she find no favour in his eyes, because he hath found some unseemly thing in her, that he shall write her a bill of divorcement, and give it in her hand, and send her out of his house.

And when she is departed out of his house, she may go and be another man's wife.

[1] All quotations from the Bible given in the Report are from the Revised Version.

The school of Rabbi Hillel interpreted the term "some unseemly thing" in a very wide sense, so that a man might divorce his wife on trivial grounds, whereas the school of Rabbi Shammai restricted the "unseemly thing" solely to the sin of adultery. In the Matthean passages, therefore, our Lord is reported as agreeing with Shammai against Hillel, and in both Matt. 5. 32 and 19. 9 as allowing one exception to the permanence of the marriage bond. Further, in both places the Matthean version seems to imply that our Lord accepted the Jewish discrimination against women in matrimonial affairs, for the right of divorce is allowed to the man only. This agrees with the Lucan saying; but conflicts both with St Paul's Dominical teaching in 1 Cor. 7. 10,[1] which implies a knowledge of the teaching behind the Marcan version, and also with the New Testament principle that men and women are equal in the sight of God. For this reason, among others, and because they are inconsistent with the statements in St Mark and St Luke, the two exceptive clauses in St Matthew are not regarded now by the generality of scholars as part of the original teaching of our Lord. Although there is strong evidence that they form part of the original text of St Matthew's Gospel they require explanation. We refrain, however, from entering upon the important question as to whether here, and elsewhere, our Lord's "I say unto you" means that he is legislating, or stating a principle which for Christians has an absolute character. To discuss this difficult and complicated question adequately would take us too far from the main subject.

As the usual word for adultery is *moicheia*, it has been suggested that in the context of the exceptive clauses, *porneia* might mean either pre-nuptial unchastity or relations within the prohibited degrees. If either of these is the correct interpretation, the exceptive clauses would refer to conditions existing before, or at the time of, the marriage, and not to something that occurred after the marriage, that is, to grounds of what we should call nullity rather than to grounds of divorce. But the suggestion is difficult to sustain, and "the preponderance of opinion seems to be clearly in favour of the view that *porneia* in the two passages mentioned means unchastity generally, with special reference to post-marital unfaithfulness . . . persisted in to a point where it has become a virtual renunciation of the original marriage."[2]

Summing up, we may say that in the Church of England teaching about marriage in recent years has been much influenced by the progress of Gospel criticism, which, as we have seen, leads to the conclusion that the exceptive clauses in St Matthew's Gospel do not form part of the original teaching of

---

[1] See p. 5.

[2] *Church and Marriage* Report (1935), p. 67. This opinion was confirmed by the two scholars whom we consulted; see Appendices 7 and 8, pp. 61 and 67 below.

our Lord. Resolution 39 of the Lambeth Conference of 1908 shows that at that date the majority of Anglican bishops regarded themselves as bound by what were then considered to be our Lord's words to recognize divorce in the case of fornication or adultery.[1] The Joint Committee of the Convocations in 1935 on *The Church and Marriage*, though insisting that the exceptive clause was part of the original text of St Matthew and that in a study of the total New Testament teaching on marriage "its preservation in the Canonical Scriptures cannot be disregarded", yet reported that "it is the almost unanimous opinion of the scholars consulted that the 'exceptive clause' in Matt. V. 32 and XIX. 9 is in neither place part of the original teaching of our Lord." This conclusion is now generally accepted, although the exceptive clause records how at least one early Christian community interpreted our Lord's teaching on marriage, believing that they were acting according to his mind.

We now turn to the evidence of the Epistles. St Paul repeats our Lord's prohibition of divorce:

> But unto the married I give charge, yea not I, but the Lord, That the wife depart not from her husband (but and if she depart, let her remain unmarried, or else be reconciled to her husband); and that the husband leave not his wife.
>
> (1 Cor. 7. 10–11.)

He continues, however, with a passage which, though difficult of interpretation, has been of some importance in the administration of Christian marriage discipline:

> But to the rest say I, not the Lord: If any brother hath an unbelieving wife, and she is content to dwell with him, let him not leave her.
>
> And the woman which hath an unbelieving husband, and he is content to dwell with her, let her not leave her husband.

---

[1] Resolution 39 of the Lambeth Conference of 1908:

"This Conference reaffirms the resolutions of the Conference of 1888 as follows:

(a) That inasmuch as our Lord's words expressly forbid divorce, except in case of fornication or adultery, the Christian Church cannot recognize divorce in any other than the excepted case, or give any sanction to the marriage of any person who has been divorced contrary to this law, during the life of the other party.

(b) That under no circumstances ought the guilty party, in the case of a divorce for fornication or adultery, to be regarded, during the life-time of the innocent party, as a fit recipient of the blessing of the Church on marriage.

(c) That, recognizing the fact that there always has been a difference of opinion in the Church on the question whether our Lord meant to forbid marriage to the innocent party in a divorce for adultery, the Conference recommends that the clergy should not be instructed to refuse the Sacraments or other privileges of the Church to those who, under civil sanction, are thus married."

For the unbelieving husband is sanctified in the wife, and the unbelieving wife is sanctified in the brother: else were your children unclean; but now are they holy. Yet if the unbelieving departeth, let him depart: the brother or the sister is not under bondage in such cases: but God hath called us in peace.

For how knowest thou, O wife, whether thou shalt save thy husband? or how knowest thou, O husband, whether thou shalt save thy wife?

Only, as the Lord hath distributed to each man, as God hath called each, so let him walk. And so ordain I in all the churches.

(1 Cor. 7. 12–17.)

The traditional interpretation of the passage is that when one of two unbelieving partners to a marriage is converted to the Christian religion and the remaining unbelieving partner is not content to dwell peaceably with the Christian convert, the latter is free to contract a new marriage with another Christian. Two things are clear and definite. First, that St Paul is here giving his own opinion on a practical issue concerning which he has no applicable saying of the Lord (cf. 1 Cor. 7, 8, 9, 12). Secondly, that he holds that a Christian convert is not bound to community of life with a pagan partner if the latter is unwilling to dwell with the convert. It is not, however, so certain that the Christian partner is set free to marry again. Such would, in many ways, seem the most natural interpretation of the passage, for otherwise it is not easy to see why the matter should be discussed at such length. It is the interpretation supported by the bulk of Christian tradition. St Paul does not say explicitly that the departure of the pagan partner leaves the convert free to marry again. It has, however, been for many centuries the practice in the greater part of Christendom to interpret the words "the brother or the sister is not under bondage in such cases" as meaning that he or she is free to marry again. The principle is clearly of great importance in the work of the Church, particularly in pagan countries. It is technically known as "the Pauline privilege".

Assuming that this is a correct interpretation of St Paul's words, what is its explanation? The Apostle, like other New Testament writers, is acutely conscious of having been transferred from one sphere or state of life called variously the world, bondage, or darkness, to a new life which is the realm of grace, freedom, and light. The Christian is one who has passed from death to life, who from being a "natural" man has become a "spiritual" man. This change is brought about through incorporation into Christ, and it affects all human activities. Henceforth these are to be carried on "in the Lord" (1 Cor. 7. 39; 15. 58; Col. 3. 17; 4. 17) or "in the Spirit" (Gal. 5. 16–26). Later ages were to speak of an order of redemption, by contrast with an order of creation or an order of fallen humanity. The New Testament gives full justification for describing the order of redemption as a new creation in which the original purposes of God, obscured and temporarily defeated in the corruption of human history, are once more made plain. In the new creation men are, through his grace, put in the way of fulfilling God's original purposes, entering here on earth an existence which can be called the Kingdom of God and eternal life. In this state the true doctrine of marriage, as of other natural relationships, is restored. As Dr Farrer writes: "Christ derived his law of marriage from the creation of man, treating Moses's ordinance as a secondary thing, accommodated to man's corrupt state."[1] St Paul appears to carry this teaching to the extent of holding that Christian marriage has a permanence and indissolubility which do not necessarily belong to pagan marriage. He is firmly opposed to the marriage of a Christian with an unbeliever (2 Cor. 6.14). It seems to be this sharp distinction that he makes between the sphere of fallen human nature and the order of redemption which leads him to allow in circumstances already mentioned the dissolution of a pagan marriage when one of the partners becomes a Christian. The Pauline privilege is all the more remarkable when we consider the Apostle's emphasis on the reality and permanence of the relationship which even an illicit union produces. "Or know ye not that he that is joined to a harlot is one body? for, The twain, saith he, shall become one flesh." (1 Cor. 6. 16.) Here the text of Genesis 2. 24, quoted by our Lord in connection with the closeness of the marriage bond (Mark 10. 7, 8), is applied to extra-marital relations. This application emphasizes the full iniquity of carnal sin as an illicit union involving the whole personality. It also emphasizes the importance of the consecration of the whole man to be indwelt by God.

The drawing of this parallel between an earthly relationship and the relation of the Lord to the believer foreshadows the language of the Epistle to the Ephesians (whether we regard that Epistle as being by St Paul himself or another writer under Pauline influence). In Ephesians 4, 5, and 6, the relationship of Christ to the Christian and to the Church is used over and over again as a model or pattern for the behaviour of Christians to one another. Thus in Chapter 4, the unity, order, and peace of the members of the Body of Christ (verses 1–16) are the basis of an exhortation to Christians to speak the truth and to deal honestly by their neighbours (verses 25–32); and in Chapter 6 servants are told to regard the service of Christ as the model of the service which they should give to their earthly masters (verses 5–9). The second part of Chapter 5 deals with the relation of

[1] *A Study in St Mark*, p. 287.

husband and wife, and here the relation of Christ and the Church is used as the model. As the Church is subject to Christ, so wives ought to be to their husbands, and as Christ loved the Church and gave himself up for it, so ought men also to love their wives. At this point, the writer seems to move from one union to the other and back again, saying at one time that the union of husband and wife helps to an understanding of the union of Christ and the Church, and then that the union of Christ and the Church shows what the union of husband and wife should be. He quotes the text of Gen. 2. 24 ("Therefore shall a man leave his father and his mother, and shall cleave unto his wife: and they shall be one flesh"), and continues: "This mystery is great: but I speak in regard of Christ and of the church." (Verse 32.) The relation between Christ and his Church is the reality, the piece of truth which we know, and we must use it as an aid to understand what we see less truly, namely the proper relationship of husband and wife, the true meaning of "becoming one flesh".

The term "mystery", however, needs further comment. Elsewhere in the Epistle to the Ephesians (1. 9–10; 3. 3–6; 3. 9; 6. 19) the mystery is the hidden purpose of God now made known—namely "the unification of humanity in the Christ, the new human hope, a hope for all men of all conditions, a hope not for men only but even for the universe".[1] We must conclude, therefore, that the "mystery" is the close personal union between man and man or between race and race in the order of redemption, a union that finds its highest expression in the relation between Christ and his Church. Of this union the order of creation provides a close parallel and an illuminating symbol, in the sexual union of man and wife. Subsequent interpretation of this passage strongly influenced the conception of marriage as a sacrament. In the Vulgate the Greek *mysterion* is translated by the Latin *sacramentum*. The term *sacramentum* was applied to the statement on marriage which precedes it rather than to the phrase that follows it. This was sufficient to encourage theologians to suppose that there was direct Biblical authority for regarding marriage as a sacrament. With the sacramental nature of marriage we shall deal more fully in the next section.

We are aware that the Matthean exception and the Pauline privilege can be explained as the action of the Church, under the guidance of the Holy Spirit, exercising its authority to "bind and loose", and so adjusting its discipline to meet the contemporary situation and the spiritual needs of those who have failed to live up to the standard of marriage enjoined by Christ. When due allowance has been made for this, we are unanimous in our opinion that in the New Testament the principle of the permanence of the

[1] J. Armitage Robinson, *St Paul's Epistle to the Ephesians*, p. 239.

marriage bond is unequivocally affirmed. It is recognized that in the old dispensation Moses permitted divorce as an accommodation to the fallen state of man; but "Jesus came preaching a Kingdom in which God's will was accepted and by which men's hearts were turned",[1] and in this new dispensation the divine order is made plain again and marriage is shown to be the permanent union described in Gen. 2. 24. This teaching the Church of England accepts without reservation. We have already noted its exposition in the Book of Common Prayer. It has been reiterated in a number of official statements, of which the following are characteristic:

Act of the Convocations, June 1938:

That this House affirms that according to God's will declared by our Lord, marriage is in its true principle a personal union, for better or for worse, of one man with one woman, exclusive of all others on either side, and indissoluble save by death.[2]

Lambeth Conference Resolution 1920, confirmed in 1930:

The Conference affirms (reaffirms) as our Lord's principle and standard of marriage a life-long and indissoluble union, for better, for worse, of one man with one woman, to the exclusion of all others on either side.[3]

The Civil Law of England is to the same effect:

Marriage is the voluntary union for life of one man and one woman to the exclusion of all others.[4]

3. *The Sacramental Nature of Marriage*

The question whether marriage is or is not a sacrament has been given special importance because it has been alleged that the idea that marriage is indissoluble would never have been put forward if the Church had not proclaimed marriage a sacrament. We believe this allegation to be without foundation. The traditional Christian teaching is that marriage is a permanent union, not only by Christian law, but also by the natural order established by God from the beginning.[5] Our Lord taught that from the beginning man and woman were by marriage made "one flesh".

[1] C. H. Dodd and A. Richardson, "Marriage and the Family in the New Testament", in *Education for Christian Marriage*, ed. A. S. Nash (1939), p. 62.

[2] *Acts of the Convocations of Canterbury and York*, ed. Smethurst and Wilson, S.P.C.K., 1948, p. 90.

[3] Resolution 67 of the Lambeth Conference of 1920, confirmed by Resolution 11 of the Lambeth Conference of 1930.   Cf. *Lambeth Conference 1948*, p. 98.

[4] *Hyde* v. *Hyde* (1866), L. R. 1 P. & D. 130, at p. 133 *per* Lord Penzance.

[5] Matt. 19. 4–6.   "And he answered and said, Have ye not read, that he which made them from the beginning made them male and female, and said, For this cause shall a man leave his father and mother, and shall cleave to his wife; and the twain shall become one flesh? So that they are no more twain, but one flesh. What therefore God hath joined together, let not man put asunder."

There can, however, be no doubt that the strength of the case for the permanence of the marriage tie is reinforced by the teaching that marriage is a sacrament. That marriage is a sacrament is the view both of the Roman and of the Orthodox Churches. Whether it can be held in the Anglican Communion is disputed. Article XXV excludes all but two—Baptism and the Lord's Supper—from the list of sacraments of the Gospel. At the same time it is not disputed among the members of the Commission that marriage partakes of "the nature of a sacrament".

St Augustine says that a sacrament is a holy sign:[1] the Catechism defines it as "an outward and visible sign of an inward and spiritual grace, given unto us, ordained by Christ Himself, as a means whereby we receive the same and a pledge to assure us thereof." Matrimony partakes of the nature of a sacrament because "in it is signified and represented the spiritual marriage and unity betwixt Christ and his Church."[2] Matrimony having no "visible sign or ceremony ordained of God",[3] its efficient cause is the mutual consent of persons lawfully capable of contracting matrimony to give themselves to each other in order to become "one flesh", and its form is the mutual declaration of such consent made by each of the parties to a marriage. The grace proper to itself given in matrimony is that whereby the parties to a marriage are sanctified, and are enabled to live faithfully together according to their vow, to bring up their children in the fear and nurture of the Lord and to maintain their union so long as they both shall live.

Our conclusion therefore is that even though marriage is not accounted a sacrament of the Gospel by Article XXV, it nevertheless partakes of the character of a sacrament, of which the parties are themselves the ministers.

From time to time it has been argued that some particular sign, e.g., the joining of hands or the giving of a ring or rings, is of the essence of a form of marriage. The arguments have not found general acceptance in the Church. It has also been argued that the benediction pronounced by the priest before whom the contract is made is of the essence of the form of marriage, or that the priest before whom the marriage takes place is the minister of the sacrament. This is not so. The generally accepted view of Western Christendom has been that the parties are themselves the ministers and that no priestly benediction is necessary for the validity of the marriage.

1 St Augustine, *De Civitate Dei*, 10.5: "Sacrificium ergo visibile invisibilis sacrificii sacramentum, id est sacrum signum, est." ("A sacrifice therefore is the visible sacrament or sacred sign of an invisible sacrifice.")

2 Book of Common Prayer: Form of Solemnization of Matrimony.

3 Article XXV.

4. *The Essential Elements in Marriage*

During the history of the Church two different things have been held to be the essential factor in true marriage, namely, consent and consummation. The doctrine that "consummation" was the essential factor seems to have resulted partly at least from the parallel drawn between the union of Christ with the Church and the union of the flesh (*commixtio carnis*) of husband and wife, and was maintained by a number of theologians and canonists. In the course of the twelfth century, however, the doctrine of the Roman Civil Law that (in the absence of impediments) consent, not consummation, makes a marriage (*matrimonium consensus non concubitus facit*) was established. The doctrine that consummation makes the marriage has left a mark on Roman Catholic Canon Law in the teaching that an unconsummated marriage (*matrimonium non consummatum*) can be dissolved by the Pope[1]; and it is plain that so long as a marriage remains unconsummated there is always the possibility that it may be annulled on grounds of impotence. With this in mind, therefore, we would say that the consummation of marriage imparts to it the highest degree of firmness, though it is now agreed that consent is the true essential. The Church's teaching is that marriage is constituted by the free and deliberate consent of the parties concerned. When that is once given between a man and a woman whose union is not barred by any impediment, the contract is made. It will, therefore, be necessary for us, after examining the Civil Law of Marriage, historically and as it is at the present day, to consider in Chapter IV the whole subject of what constitutes true matrimonial consent, and in Chapter V the place which consummation occupies in relation to the law of Nullity.

[1] *Codex Juris Canonici*, Canon 1119.

CHAPTER II

THE HISTORICAL RELATIONSHIP BETWEEN THE ECCLESIASTICAL AND CIVIL LAW OF MARRIAGE

1. *The Early Church*

IN THE polity of the early Church moral disputes between Christians were required to be settled by the bishop and other officers of the local church.[1] Roman law recognized a procedure by which two litigants, instead of going to the ordinary Courts, could choose an arbitrator whose decision would be enforced by the praetor. These two procedures, Christian custom and Roman law, appear to be the basis of the incorporation of episcopal Courts into the judicial system of the Empire by the Christian emperors in the fourth century. Any person might remove his case at any stage from a Civil Court to that of the bishop, even against the will of his opponent, and in the episcopal Court the bishop decided the matter according to his own conception of right and wrong and without appeal.[2] From the earliest times it had been insisted that marriage cases between Christians were the concern of the Church. Thus about A.D. 115 St Ignatius writes to Polycarp, Bishop of Smyrna: "It becometh men and women too, when they marry, to unite themselves with the consent of the Bishop, that the marriage may be after the Lord and not after concupiscence."[3] From the fourth century they fell to be decided under the procedure just described.

The Roman Civil Law of Marriage continued for the most part as it had been before the conversion of Constantine, but the Church Courts increasingly enforced their own conception of marriage among Christians.

2. *The Eastern Church*

In the Orthodox Church of the East the tradition has been from early times to accept State legislation about marriage and divorce. From the ninth century onwards in the Byzantine Empire imperial legislation made the Church's blessing of the matrimonial contract the legally constitutive element in marriage. In Greece the Civil Courts have exclusive jurisdiction in

---

[1] The *Apostolic Constitutions* show a well-developed system for the administration of justice in such matters.

[2] The privilege was confirmed by the Emperors Arcadius and Honorius in A.D. 398 and by Honorius and Theodosius II in 408.

[3] *Epistle of Ignatius to Polycarp*, cap. 5.

matrimonial causes; but in divorce proceedings a period is allotted during which the bishop allows separation *a mensa et thoro* as a temporary measure, and uses his efforts to reconcile the two parties. In some other countries, such as Turkey, where the State has not regulated procedure in such cases, the Church has its own Courts to deal with them.[1]

3. *The West during the Middle Ages*

In the barbarian kingdoms which established themselves after the fall of the Western Empire, the secular power continued to legislate and adjudicate on marriage down to the tenth century and the Church continued also to have its own tribunals. The greater ecclesiastics, however, acquired more and more influence in the government of these kingdoms, and were able to bring civil legislation into closer accord with Christian principles, while the disciplinary authority of the Church became more effective. In the course of the tenth century in Italy and in France this process resulted in the acquisition by the Church of sole and complete jurisdiction over marriage cases.

In England, before the Norman Conquest, the bishop and the earl sat side by side in Court as joint judges of all suits, both ecclesiastical and secular.[2] But the Church came to insist that marriage was a matter of which she alone should have cognizance, since marriage was an aspect of morals.[3] After the Norman Conquest the ecclesiastical and civil jurisdictions were separated,[4] and the Ecclesiastical Courts became the only Courts with jurisdiction to determine whether a marriage was valid or void.[5] Questions arising in the Courts of Common Law as to the validity of a marriage were sent to the bishop for trial.[6] Further, any party to a marriage, or anyone with an interest in determining the validity of a marriage, could petition the bishop independently for judgement in the matter.[7] Finally, the Ecclesiastical Court could proceed on its own authority to declare a purported marriage null and void and to separate the spouses; e.g., if they were within the prohibited degrees of relationship.[8]

The basis of the law administered by the Ecclesiastical Courts was the

[1] On the history and practice of the Eastern Church in these matters see: Hamilcar Alivisatos, *Marriage and Divorce in accordance with the Canon Law of the Orthodox Church*, a lecture given in the University of London, 5 July 1948, and published by the Faith Press, Ltd.

[2] 3 Edgar c.5, cited in Robertson, *Laws of the Kings of England*, p. 27.

[3] Pollock and Maitland, *Hist. of English Law*, Vol. II. p. 366.

[4] Ordinance of William I, 1070–6, cited Stubbs, *Select Charters*, 9th ed., p. 99.

[5] Pollock and Maitland, op. cit., p. 367.

[6] Glanvill, Lib. VII, c. 13, 14.

[7] See, e.g., *Act Book of the Ecclesiastical Court of Whalley*, ed. A. M. Cooke, Cheetham Soc. N.S., vol. 44, p. 28.

[8] Esmein, *Mariage en Droit Canonique*, 2nd ed., Vol. I, p. 455.

general Canon Law of the Western Church as it came to be codified in the *Corpus Juris Canonici*. It has been in recent times a matter of controversy as to the extent to which this body of law was binding on the English Ecclesiastical Courts; but it is now generally accepted by historians that the matrimonial law of England before the Reformation is to be found in the component parts of the *Corpus Juris Canonici* and the commentaries thereon.[1]

In the Middle Ages (and indeed thereafter) the term divorce (*divortium*) was used in two senses:

(a) *divortium a vinculo* in cases of Nullity, where the Court declared the parties never to have been married and therefore each to be free to marry another;

(b) *divortium a mensa et thoro*, where, in cases of adultery and cruelty, the Court pronounced a decree of Separation, but the marriage tie subsisted.

Divorce, in the modern sense of the term, was known to the pre-Reformation Canon Law only in the case of the Papal dissolution of an unconsummated marriage.

Grounds for Nullity of Marriage (*divortium a vinculo*) under the Canon Law were set out by Tancred in the thirteenth century as follows:

> Error, conditio, votum, cognatio, crimen,
> Cultus disparitas, vis, ordo, ligamen, honestas,
> Dissensus, et affinis, si clandestinus et impos,
> Raptave sit mulier, loco nec reddita tuto,
> Haec facienda vetant connubia, facta retractant.

These grounds were all *impedimenta dirimenta* (absolute bars) which rendered the marriage void; but the lines do not include all the grounds for nullity contained in the *Corpus Juris*, as will be seen from the summary, set out in Appendix 5,[2] of grounds of nullity under the Canon Law.

4. *The Legal Effect of the Reformation*

The same Ecclesiastical Courts continued to have cognizance of matrimonial suits after the Reformation as before it. Appeals, however, no longer

---

[1] E.g., F. W. Maitland, *Canon Law in the Church of England*; Pollock and Maitland, op. cit., Vol. I, pp. 111–35, Vol. II, pp. 364–98; H. W. C. Davis, *The Canon Law in England*, reprinted in J. R. H. Weaver and A. L. Poole, *Henry William Carless Davis*, p. 923; Z. N. Brooke, *The English Church and the Papacy*, 1931; *The Canon Law of the Church of England*, 1947, pp. 36 *et seq*. Bishop Stubbs himself by the end of his life came a considerable way to meet this view: see his *Lectures on Mediaeval and Modern History*, 3rd Ed., pp. 335–6.

[2] See Appendix 5, page 57 below.

lay from the Court of Arches or the Chancery Court of York (the Ecclesiastical Courts of Appeal) to the Pope, but to a Court of Delegates appointed *ad hoc* by the Crown.[1] The law administered by the Ecclesiastical Courts was the traditional Canon Law of the Church together with the legislation of the medieval popes.[2] But this body of law was modified in three main directions. First, by a legislative fiction[3] the canons were declared to have always been received in England as "customary law": this left the Courts free to reject any provision held not to be reasonable or equitable. Secondly, the canons were expressly made subject to "the law, statutes and customs of this realm".[4] Thirdly, there was a rigorous curtailment of the prohibited degrees of matrimony.

The result was that the only Courts empowered after the Reformation, as before, to declare a marriage valid or void were the Ecclesiastical Courts; and the basis of the law which they applied was to be found in the appropriate sections of the *Corpus Juris Canonici* and the Commentaries thereon. On the other hand, the Ecclesiastical Courts were bound to apply such modifications of the Canon Law as were enacted by the legislature; and were also subject to the interference of the Common Law Courts by writ of prohibition when those Courts considered that the Ecclesiastical Courts were infringing some principle of the Common or Statute Law, or were exceeding their jurisdiction.

5. *The Development of a Distinction between Void and Voidable Marriages*

The pre-Reformation Canon Law knew no distinction between void and voidable marriages: marriages were either void or valid. It did, however, draw a distinction between an impediment to a marriage which rendered it wholly void (*impedimentum dirimens*) and an impediment to a marriage which left it wholly valid but rendered the parties subject to ecclesiastical censure or punishment (*impedimentum prohibitivum*). The effect of a decree annulling a marriage on the ground of an *impedimentum dirimens* was to bastardize the offspring. The Ecclesiastical Courts would pronounce such a decree at the suit of an interested person, even though the parties to the marriage in

---

[1] The composition varied, but almost always included some of the civilians from Doctors' Commons. A full commission in 1781 consisted of three spiritual lords, three temporal lords, three judges of the Common Law Courts and three civilians; see *Harford* v. *Morris* (1776), 2 Hag. Con. 423, at p. 436. By 1832 in ordinary cases the Court consisted of three puisne judges and three civilians; see Holdsworth, *Hist. of English Law*, 5th Ed., Vol. I, p. 605, and *Report of the Commission on Ecclesiastical Courts*, 1832, Special Report 6.

[2] *The Canon Law of the Church of England*, 1947, p. 47.

[3] (1533), Act for the Submission of the Clergy, 25 Hen. 8, c. 19, ss. 3, 7; (1543), 35 Hen. 8, c. 16, s. 3.

[4] (1533), 25 Hen. 8, c. 19.

question were dead. The principal dirimentary impediments on which the Ecclesiastical Courts acted in this way were:

(i) a prior existing marriage or espousal of one of the parties;

(ii) impotence;

(iii) prohibited degrees of relationship;

(iv) absence of true consent.

The Courts of Common Law recognized that where one of the parties to a purported marriage had a spouse still living, the purported marriage must always be void and the offspring illegitimate; bigamy was a crime cognizable by the Common Law Courts from 1603.[1] Similarly, the Common Law Courts recognized absence of consent or infancy as vitiating an ostensible contract. But so far as other dirimentary impediments were concerned the Courts of Common Law made a distinction. They recognized that while the parties to a purported marriage were still living together the Church was entitled through her Courts to separate the parties *pro salute animae*. But once the purported marriage had been effectively dissolved by death this reason disappeared: the Courts of Common Law therefore intervened in such a case by writ of prohibition to prevent the Ecclesiastical Courts declaring the marriage void and the offspring, by necessary implication, illegitimate. This led to a distinction between civil and canonical disabilities. With regard to the former (i.e., bigamy, non-age, or absence of consent), the Ecclesiastical Courts could, at any time, at the suit of any interested party, declare the marriage void. But where there was a canonical disability (i.e., a dirimentary impediment other than bigamy, non-age, or absence of consent) the Ecclesiastical Courts could only annul the marriage during the lifetime of both parties. The result was that the validity of a marriage subject to a canonical disability became indisputable once one party thereto was dead; and by further development a marriage subject to a canonical disability came to be regarded as valid until annulled. Marriages subject to a civil disability were therefore *void ab initio*: marriages subject to a canonical disability were *voidable* only during the lifetime of the parties.[2]

6. *Principal Statutory Modifications before 1857*

By the Marriage of Lunatics Act, 1742,[3] the marriage of a lunatic so found by inquisition,[4] even during a lucid interval, was rendered null and void. By

---

[1] 1 Jac. 1, c. 11.

[2] See, for this paragraph, *Elliott* v. *Gurr* (1812), 2 Phillim. 16; *Ray* v. *Sherwood* (1836), 1 Curt. 173, 188; *A.* v. *B.* (1868), L. R. 1 P. & D. 559. In the case of impotence, the marriage was voidable only at the suit of the parties themselves.

[3] 15 Geo. 2, c. 30, repealed and substantially re-enacted by the Marriage of Lunatics Act, 1811 (51 Geo. 3, c. 37).

[4] The procedure, although available, is now obsolescent (see p. 21).

Lord Hardwicke's Act, 1753,[1] certain preliminaries by way of publicizing an impending marriage were made essential to its validity; and a subsisting espousal to a third person was abolished as a ground for annulling a marriage. By the Marriage Act, 1835,[2] marriages between persons related within the prohibited degrees of consanguinity or affinity, which had previously been voidable,[3] were made void *ab initio*. Each of these Statutes, as well as the distinction between void and voidable marriages, involved an invasion and modification of the preceding Ecclesiastical Law of Marriage and Nullity: nevertheless each was accepted and enforced by the Church Courts.[4]

7. *The Matrimonial Causes Act, 1857*

By the Matrimonial Causes Act, 1857,[5] jurisdiction in matrimonial causes was taken away from the Ecclesiastical Courts, and vested in a new secular Court, the Court for Divorce and Matrimonial Causes.[6] By section 22 the new Court was to act in all suits other than those to dissolve the marriage (including therefore suits for Annulment) on the same principles and rules as those in use in the superseded Ecclesiastical Courts.[7]

8. *Main Statutory Modifications since 1857*

By the Deceased Wife's Sister's Marriage Act, 1907,[8] and subsequent Statutes of analogous import,[9] the prohibited degrees of relationship were modified: and the Church of England made similar modifications in its canons in May 1946.[10] It should be noted that the Deceased Wife's Sister's Marriage Act, 1907, did not merely repeal the statutory prohibition of marriage with a deceased wife's sister (32 Hen. 8, c. 38): it enacted that no

[1] 26 Geo. 2, c. 33.

[2] 5 & 6 Will. 4, c. 54.

[3] See p. 16.

[4] See, e.g., *Turner* v. *Meyers* (1808), 1 Hag. Con. 414, at p. 417 (Marriage of Lunatics Act, 1742); *Brealy* v. *Reed* (1841), 2 Curt. 833 (Marriage Act, 1823, which replaced Lord Hardwicke's Act, 1753); *Brook* v. *Brook* (1861), 9 H. L. C. 193 (Marriage Act, 1835); *Elliott* v. *Gurr* (1812), 2 Phillim. 16 (voidable marriages).

[5] 20 & 21 Vict. c. 85.

[6] Ibid., s. 6. This Court was itself merged in the High Court of Justice in 1873 (Supreme Court of Judicature Act, 1873, 36 & 37 Vict. c. 66, s. 16).

[7] Matrimonial Causes Act, 1857, s. 22, was repealed by s. 226 and the Sixth Schedule of the Supreme Court of Judicature (Consolidation) Act, 1925, but was in substance re-enacted by s. 32 of that Act: see *Baxter* v. *Baxter*, [1948] A. C. 274, at p. 285 *per* Lord Jowitt, L.C.

[8] 7 Edw. 7, c. 47.

[9] Deceased Brother's Widow's Marriage Act, 1921; Marriage (Prohibited Degrees of Relationship) Act, 1931. These Acts and the 1907 Act were repealed and re-enacted by the Marriage Act, 1949, ss. 1, 79, and First and Fifth Schedules. (See Appendix 1, p. 49 below.)

[10] Revised Canon XCIX, enacted on 21 May 1946, by the Convocation of Canterbury, and 22 May 1946, by the Convocation of York: see *Chronicle of Convocation*, May 1946, pp. iv, v.

such marriage "shall be deemed to have been or shall be void or voidable, *as a civil contract*, by reason only of such affinity", and by a further provision it afforded relief to the Clergy of the Church of England in respect of the alteration thereby made. In this Statute the Legislature for the first time seems to have recognized a distinction between the civil and ecclesiastical aspects of marriage, and to have altered the law in a civil sense only, without purporting to affect the Ecclesiastical Law. However, no such distinction is now to be found in the Marriage Act, 1949, by which the Statute 32 Hen. 8, 1540, c. 38, and the Deceased Wife's Sister's Marriage Act, 1907, have both been repealed.

Modifications have also been made relating to the hours during which marriage might lawfully be celebrated[1]; here again the canons of the Church of England were similarly modified.[2] By the Age of Marriage Act, 1929,[3] the age at which persons might lawfully marry was raised from 14 years in the case of a male and 12 years in the case of a female to 16 years in the case of both:[4] draft canons now before Convocation are intended to bring the Ecclesiastical Law into line.[5] Finally, the Matrimonial Causes Act, 1937, s. 7,[6] established a number of new grounds which render a marriage voidable.[7]

9. *Conclusion*

It is apparent from the foregoing that until 1857 the Civil and Ecclesiastical Laws of Marriage were identical. So far as nullity is concerned, the only possible statutory divergence since then[8] arises out of the Age of Marriage Act, 1929,[9] and the Matrimonial Causes Act, 1937, s. 7.[10] Finally, judicial interpretation of the law since 1857, except in so far as it relates to new statutory grounds of nullity, purports to be no more than an elucidation of the Church Law of Marriage as it existed before 1857.[11]

---

1 Marriage Act, 1886; Marriage (Extension of Hours) Act, 1934; repealed and re-enacted by the Marriage Act, 1949, ss. 4, 79 and Fifth Sched.

2 Amended Canons LXII and CII, enacted 27 May 1936; see *Chronicle of Convocation*, May 1936, p. xviii and Appendix.

3 19 & 20, Geo. 5, c. 36; repealed and re-enacted by the Marriage Act, 1949, ss. 2, 79, and Fifth Sched. (See Appendix 1, p. 49 below.)

4 At Common Law a child aged 7 years or more was deemed capable of giving an inchoate consent, which could be withdrawn when a boy reached 14 or a girl 12 years of age.

5 Draft Canon XXXVIII, cl. 3.

6 1 Edw. 8 & 1 Geo. 6, c. 58, repealed and re-enacted by Matrimonial Causes Act, 1950, s. 8. (See Appendix 1, p. 49 below.)

7 See p. 23.

8 Unless the granting of divorce, with right to re-marry, by Act of Parliament, is to be regarded as constituting a divergence.

9 Now Marriage Act, 1949, s. 2. See Appendix 1, p. 49 below.

10 Now Matrimonial Causes Act, 1950, s. 8. See Appendix 1, p. 49 below.

11 See *Baxter* v. *Baxter*, [1948] A. C. 274, at p. 285 *per* Lord Jowitt, L.C.

CHAPTER III

THE PRESENT CIVIL LAW OF NULLITY

1. *The Nature of Marriage in Civil Law*

IN ORDER to understand the impediments to a valid marriage, it must first be understood what marriage means in Civil Law. Marriage may be defined as the legal relationship which is created by an immediate contract sanctioned by law between one man and one woman to live together during their joint lives to the exclusion of all others. The law envisages that this living-together is on terms (in general) of connubial intercourse with a view to raising a family. The contract of marriage results in each party having the status of a married person and their children having the status of legitimacy.

2. *Void and Voidable Marriages*

We have already[1] traced historically how a distinction arose between void and voidable marriages. It falls now to consider their juridical differences in modern English law.

A void marriage is a marriage subject to such a defect as to fail in its primary intentions and primary legal effect; that is, it fails to confer on either of the parties the status of married person with a right to *consortium*.[2] It is in theory unnecessary to have recourse to the Courts for the annulment of a void marriage: it fails in its legal effect irrespective of any decree. One or other of the parties, however, frequently does seek a decree of Annulment of the marriage, if only because some defect to which it is subject may be disputed and likely as time passes to become more difficult of proof, or because it is desired to establish the nullity beyond all question in order to permit marriage to another party or at any rate to establish the right of a party to single status.

In the case of a voidable marriage it is necessary to apply to the Court to

---

[1] See paragraph 5, pp. 15 *et seq.*

[2] A void marriage now has important *secondary* legal consequences which differ in no way from those produced by a valid marriage, e.g., the Court after a decree of Nullity may order the "husband" to provide for his "wife" or their children and may vary settlements. For this reason the traditional view that a void marriage is one which produces no legal effects at all (*Nullus est quod nullum producit effectum*) does not accord with modern practice: nor does the wording of the decree of Nullity pronounced by the Court, which is based on the traditional theory; see Introduction, p. ix; and *In Re Eaves*, [1940] Ch. 109, at p. 121 *per* Goddard, L.J.

have it set aside.[1] Until it is set aside it creates all the legal rights and obligations and has all the legal consequences of a valid marriage: in particular, it results in the parties having the status of married persons and the offspring having the status of legitimacy, although such rights and obligations are subject to defeasance, and are destroyed retrospectively (except for some transactions which are completed before the decree) once a decree of Nullity is pronounced.[2] A voidable marriage is therefore a marriage subject to such a defect as to be liable to fail in its primary intentions and legal effect if, but only if, one of the parties takes appropriate action in the Courts during their joint lives.

Since a voidable marriage is valid until it is set aside, a party can so act in the way of approbating the marriage as to be precluded from subsequently disputing its validity. This is often referred to as the doctrine of "insincerity".[3]

3. *The Defects which render a Marriage Void*

These fall into three groups:

(i) *Lack of consent.* Since the relationship is created by a contract, of which in its turn consensus is a pre-requisite, those matters which preclude consent invalidate the marriage. Such matters are:

(*a*) Mistake (including such fraud as induces mistake);
(*b*) Duress;
(*c*) Insanity.

The subject of consent to marry covers so wide a field that it is considered separately in the next chapter.

(ii) *Lack of due form.* Since the contract is sanctioned by law, the law insists that the consent of the parties shall be manifested in a particular form.

Generally speaking, defects in form do not invalidate marriages in England. But under Section 22 of the Marriage Act, 1823,[4] "if any persons . . . shall knowingly and wilfully inter-marry without due publication of banns or licence . . . the marriages of such persons shall be null and void." In order to render the marriage void it must be established that *both* parties knew and wilfully consented to such informal solemnization.[5] Cases in which marriages

---

1 See paragraph 5, p. 16 above.

2 The status of legitimacy of the children is, however, preserved: Matrimonial Causes Act, 1950, s. 9. This provision may perhaps be considered juridically as an application of the doctrine that in the case of voidable marriages completed transactions retain their legal validity: see *Mason* v. *Mason*, [1944] N.I. 134, at p. 163 *per* Andrews, C.J.

3 See G. v. M. (1885), 10 App. Cas. 171, at p. 186 *per* Lord Selborne, L.C.

4 4 Geo. 4, c. 76; repealed and substantially re-enacted by Marriage Act, 1949, ss. 25, 79, and Fifth Sched.

5 *R.* v. *Wroxton (Inhabitants)* (1833), 4 B. & A. 640.

after banns have been annulled under this provision have become very rare. It should be noted that the minister celebrating with knowledge of the irregularity is subject to criminal proceedings both secular and ecclesiastical.

(iii) *Lack of capacity.* Capacity is the ability to perform a legal act in such a way as to bring about the desired legal consequences.[1] Incapacity to marry therefore involves that the primary legal consequences of marriage do not ensue. Incapacities to marry fall into two groups:

(a) *Absolute incapacities*, where the party subject to the incapacity cannot marry at all. These are, first, a prior existing marriage; secondly, non-age; and thirdly, lunacy "so found".

α. Subsisting marriage

If a marriage is still subsisting when one of the parties goes through another ceremony of marriage with a third person the second ceremony is bigamous and null and void *ab initio*.

β. Non-age

A marriage is invalid if either of the parties is under 16 years of age.[2]

γ. Lunacy "so found"

One of the methods of ascertaining whether a person was of such unsoundness of mind that he should be subjected to the various incapacities attaching to lunacy was to establish an inquisition to inquire into his mental state.[3] If it was thereby declared that he was of unsound mind he was known as a lunatic "so found by inquisition", or, more shortly, a lunatic "so found". As appears above[4] he was thereafter precluded by the Marriage of Lunatics Act, 1742, 1811, from contracting a valid marriage: such a marriage was void *ab initio*. This procedure of inquisition of lunacy is still available, though obsolescent, and is to be clearly distinguished from the more usual procedure of certification, which does not prevent a person certified of unsound mind from marrying during a lucid interval.[5]

(b) *Relative incapacities*, where the person subject to the incapacity cannot marry some particular person. These are the prohibited degrees of consanguinity and affinity set out in Schedule I of the Marriage Act, 1949.[6] The

---

[1] This is a term of art in jurisprudence, and must not be confused with lack of sexual capacity, or impotence, which renders a marriage *voidable* and is dealt with on p. 22.

[2] Age of Marriage Act, 1929 (19 & 20 Geo. 5, c. 36), now re-enacted in the Marriage Act, 1949 (12 & 13 Geo. 6, c. 76), s. 2. See also *Pugh* v. *Pugh*, [1951] P. 482.

[3] An entertaining example of an inquisition of lunacy occasioned by a city tradesman's inordinate passion for fox-hunting is to be found in Surtees' *Handley Cross*.

[4] See Chapter II, p. 16.

[5] See Appendix 4, p. 55 below.

[6] See Appendix 1, p. 50 below.

former category of prohibited degrees laid down in 32 Hen. 8, c. 38, and set out in the Book of Common Prayer, had been altered by Statutes in the present century.[1] These alterations permit marriage between a man and his deceased wife's sister, between a woman and her deceased husband's brother, between a man and his deceased wife's niece or his aunt by marriage, and between a woman and her deceased husband's nephew or uncle by marriage. These alterations in no way affect the old prohibitions against marriages between people of the same blood or half-blood.

The Act of 1949[2] also re-enacted in substance the provision in the Supreme Court of Judicature (Consolidation) Act, 1925, s. 184, as amended by the Marriage (Prohibited Degrees of Relationship) Act, 1931, declaring that a man may not marry the sister or the half-sister of a wife whom he has divorced or who has divorced him during the life of the former wife, or the former wife of his brother or half-brother, whose marriage has been judicially dissolved during the brother's lifetime.

4. Defects which render a Marriage Voidable

These may be classified as those dependent on the Common Law and those created by Statute. The only surviving example of a Common Law defect is sexual impotence.[3]

If at the time of a ceremony of marriage one or both of the parties is incurably incapable of consummating the marriage, the Court may pronounce the marriage null and void on the petition of either of them. But in the case of a marriage of aged persons impotence does not necessarily render the marriage voidable.[4] The causes, manifestations, and proofs of impotence are too varied to particularize here. But incurable sterility in the man or the woman is not a ground for nullity.[5]

---

[1] Deceased Wife's Sister's Marriage Act, 1907 (7 Edw. 7, c. 47); Deceased Brother's Widow's Marriage Act, 1921 (11 & 12 Geo. 5, c. 24); Supreme Court of Judicature (Consolidation) Act, 1925 (15 & 16 Geo. 5, c. 49); Marriage (Prohibited Degrees of Relationship) Act, 1931 (21 & 22 Geo. 5, c. 31); Marriage Act, 1949 (12 & 13 Geo. 6, c. 76), s. 1 and First Sched. See Appendix 1, p. 49 below.

[2] Marriage Act, 1949, section 1, sub-section 3 and Schedule 1. See Appendix 1, p. 49 below.

[3] Obsolete defects of this category are: pre-contract, consanguinity and affinity. The two latter were made grounds for rendering the marriage *void* by the Marriage Act, 1835 (5 & 6 Will. 4, c. 54).

[4] It is generally an implied condition to the contract of marriage that each party is capable of sexual intercourse: see G. v. M. (1885), 10 App. Cas. 171, at p. 204 *per* Lord Fitzgerald. But a condition is only implied by law where it is reasonable and necessary so to do. In the case of the marriage of aged persons such a condition is unreasonable and unnecessary. In such cases, therefore, impotence does not necessarily render the marriage voidable.

[5] See D. v. A. (1845), 1 Rob. Ecc. 279, at p. 296 *per* Dr Lushington.

Statutory defects rendering a marriage voidable were laid down by the Matrimonial Causes Act, 1937, s. 7.[1] They are:

- (i) Wilful refusal to consummate the marriage.[2]
- (ii) Unsoundness of mind at the time of the marriage.[3]
- (iii) Mental defectiveness at the time of the marriage.[3]
- (iv) Recurrent fits of insanity at the time of the marriage.[3]
- (v) Recurrent fits of epilepsy at the time of the marriage.
- (vi) Venereal disease in a communicable form at the time of the marriage.[2]
- (vii) Pregnancy by some other man at the time of the marriage.[2]

All but one of these grounds arise before the marriage (*ex causa praecedenti*). The only exception is wilful refusal to consummate the marriage, which arises thereafter (*ex causa subsequenti*).

The following statutory conditions apply to grounds (ii)–(vii) above:

- (i) Ignorance by the petitioner of the facts alleged at the time of the marriage;
- (ii) Institution of proceedings within a year from the date of the marriage;
- (iii) Absence of marital intercourse with the consent of the petitioner since discovery of the existence of grounds for a decree.

These conditions may be regarded as a statutory application of the doctrine of approbation or "insincerity" discussed above.[4]

---

[1] Now Matrimonial Causes Act, 1950, s. 8 (1). See Appendix 1, p. 49 below.

[2] In these cases only the innocent or untainted party can complain.

[3] For the various ways in which insanity may be a ground for making a marriage void or voidable, see Appendix 4, p. 55 below.

[4] See p. 20.

CHAPTER IV

CONSENT AND INTENTION

1. *General*

At Common Law prior to Lord Hardwicke's Act, 1753, all that was required to constitute a valid marriage was an exchange of consents *per verba de praesenti*. In *R. v. Millis*,[1] it was held by a House of Lords evenly divided that such an exchange must be made in the presence of an ordained priest; but this decision, although binding, is generally considered to be historically inaccurate.[2] No formal words were necessary to constitute the exchange of consents: any expression which showed an intention to take the other as a spouse was sufficient. Common Law marriages cannot now take place in England: no marriage, other than in a foreign Embassy, can be lawfully solemnized in England unless the statutory requirements with regard to banns, notice, or licence and the place and time of marriage are observed.[3] Consent is still necessary to constitute a valid marriage; and the consent is the same as that required at Common Law, i.e., that each party expresses a present intention to take the other as spouse. If, therefore, for example, two persons acting in a play or film go through the words and actions of the marriage service even in the presence of an ordained priest, but without any intention to marry in reality, there is no marriage.

It has sometimes been suggested that in a Register Office marriage there is no true consent to marriage as it is understood by Christians, i.e., a lifelong union to the exclusion of all others. This is a total misconception. Until 1753[4] in England and until 1940[5] in Scotland a mere informal exchange of consents was sufficient to constitute a valid marriage, which would have been recognized as such by the Church; and there is such an exchange of consents in a Register Office marriage. In consequence of the report of the Committee on Procedure in Matrimonial Causes (1947)[6], all Registrars of Marriage were requested to bring to the notice of the parties at the time of the

---

[1] (1844), 10 Cl. and Fin. 534.

[2] See the opinion of Willes, J., in *Beamish* v. *Beamish* (1861), 9 H. L. C. 274; and Pollock and Maitland, *Hist. of Eng. Law*, Vol. II, p. 370.

[3] Exceptions are the marriages of Quakers and Jews.

[4] 26 Geo. 2, c. 33 (Lord Hardwicke's Act).

[5] Marriage (Scotland) Act, 1939.

[6] Cmd. 7024, p. 17, paragraph 29 (xiii). See also Appendix 6, p. 60 below.

marriage the fact that they were entering into a lifelong union and the solemn and binding character of the vows which they were making.

2. Factors precluding Consent

(i) *Unsoundness of mind*. A state of mind which precludes the giving of a genuine consent has always been recognized in English law as rendering the marriage entered into by a person in such condition void *ab initio*.[1]

The state of mind to be proved has been described as follows: "The question is whether the respondent was mentally capable of understanding the nature of the marriage contract, and the duties and responsibilities which it creates. . . . The mind of one of the parties may be capable of understanding the language used, but may yet be affected by such delusions, or other symptoms of insanity, as may satisfy the tribunal that there was not a real appreciation of the engagement apparently entered into."[2] Such a condition of mind may be the result of alcoholic intoxication or of disease.[3]

(ii) *Duress*. If a person is constrained to go through a ceremony by threats which destroy the reality of the consent, the marriage is void. The threats must be more than pressure which merely overbears the will: they must be such as to make the party coerced incapable of exercising his or her will at all.[4] Such cases are exceedingly rare, and the longer a union persists without complaint the more difficult it becomes to prove duress to the satisfaction of an English Court.

(iii) *Mistake*. The only sort of mistake which invalidates a marriage in English law is mistake as to the identity of the other party to the contract[5] (e.g., where the putative husband passed himself off as another man) or as to the nature of the ceremony (e.g., where it is thought simply to be a betrothal ceremony[6]). No other sort of mistake (e.g., as to the social position or fortune of the other spouse[7] or as to the system of law which will regulate the rights and duties of the spouses[8]) will invalidate a marriage. An ordinary contract is voidable if it has been induced by a wilful misrepresentation of material

1 See *Hunter* v. *Edney* (1881), 10 P. D. 93. See also Appendix 4, p. 55 below.

2 *Forster* v. *Forster* (1923), 39 T. L. R. 658, *per* Lord Merrivale, P.

3 *Sullivan* v. *Sullivan* (1818), 2 Hag. Con. 238; affirmed (1819), 3 Phillim. 45. The various ways in which mental incapacity may affect the validity of a marriage are considered in Appendix 4, p. 55 below.

4 *Scott* v. *Sebright* (1886), 12 P. D. 21: *Bartlett* v. *Rice* (1894), 72 L. T. 122.

5 *R.* v. *Millis* (1844), 10 Cl. and Fin. 534, at p. 785.

6 *Hall* v. *Hall* (1908), 24 T. L. R. 757; *Valier* v. *Valier* (1925), 133 L. T. 830; *Mehta* v. *Mehta*, [1945] 2 All E. R. 690.

7 *Sullivan* v. *Sullivan* (1818), 2 Hag. Con. 238, at p. 246.

8 *Way* v. *Way*, [1950] P. 71; on appeal, *sub nom. Kenward* v. *Kenward*, [1951] P. 124.

facts. This is not so in the case of a contract of marriage[1]; but the marriage is *void* if the fraud has induced mistake in either of the two senses described above. This accords with both medieval Canon Law and current Roman Catholic practice.[2]

3. Defective Intention and Conditional Consent

At the session of the Full Synod of the Convocation of York on 19 May 1949 a suggestion was put forward that the Church might recognize Defective Intention as a ground for Nullity of Marriage. The matter was raised during consideration of the proposed Canon XXXVI.[3]

The discussion took place in the light of a Case for Opinion submitted to Counsel by proctors from the Convocations of Canterbury and York and Counsel's Opinion thereupon.[4] It was suggested that where the parties had before marriage entered into an agreement contrary to the nature or purpose of marriage or which clearly showed a fundamental misunderstanding as to the nature of marriage, this should be accepted as a ground for a subsequent decree of Nullity.

The Roman Catholic Church recognizes Defective Intention and Conditional Consent in certain circumstances as constituting grounds of nullity. Defective Intention, in this context, relates to the internal disposition of one or both parties to a marriage, and is to be sharply distinguished from those forms of Defective Consent which are brought about by external or quasi-external forces (e.g., insanity or duress) acting upon the will. In the *Codex Juris Canonici*, Canon 1086, Section 2 states that "if either or both parties by a positive act of the will exclude marriage itself, or all right to the conjugal act, or any essential property of marriage, he contracts invalidly."[5]

Defective Intention appears to have been recognized as a possible ground for nullity in the medieval system from the time of Pope Innocent III (1198–1216), who allowed nullity in a case where a man had feigned matrimonial consent in order to overcome the scruples of a woman who would not allow him sexual intercourse without marriage.[6] This teaching was not unanimously accepted by the canonists during the following century,

---

[1] *Templeton* v. *Tyree* (1872), L.R. 2. P. & D. 420.

[2] See G. Fransen: *Le dol dans la conclusion des actes juridiques*, Louvain, 1946, p. 129.

[3] See Introduction, p. viii.

[4] See *York Journal of Convocation*, May 1949, pp. 22–33, reproducing the Case and the Opinion of Mr William Latey, now Q.C.

[5] "At si alterutra vel utraque pars positivo voluntatis actu excludat matrimonium ipsum, aut omne ius ad coniugalem actum, vel essentialem aliquam matrimonii proprietatem, invalide contrahit."

[6] See Decretals of Gregory IX, Bk. 4, Tit. 1, c. 26 (usually cited as X, iv, i. 26).

but seems to have prevailed by the end of the medieval period.[1] As Esmein points out, such teaching, though liable to cause confusion, could be defended at a time when marriage might be contracted in the most casual way by an informal exchange of consent and without the presence of witnesses. It is open to question, however, whether the doctrine can be justified in a society in which marriage must be contracted in set forms and the consent expressed in words provided by that society. In such circumstances marriage becomes in a fuller sense an institution of society, and people who marry according to the forms provided must be held bound by what they have voluntarily said and done. To depart from this principle would have disastrous results in the moral sphere and would in effect allow people to take advantage of perjury. Those who had perjured themselves by going through a form of marriage which they did not intend to be marriage would be placed in a position of advantage compared with those who had married genuinely but whose marriage had broken down.

It may be argued further that to exclude Defective Intention as a ground for nullity is to keep in line with the general doctrine of intention in the sacraments. Article XXVI speaks of "the Unworthiness of the Minister, which hinders not the effect of the Sacrament", and the same principle has generally been held to apply to his intention. The Roman Catholic writer Adrian Fortescue says: "A man may have utterly wrong, heretical and blasphemous views about a sacrament and yet confer or receive it quite validly."[2] The case of marriage is complicated by the fact that the parties are both the ministers and the subjects of the sacrament; but the principle would seem to hold good that their intention must be collected from the words of the rite which they employ and not from any private intentions which they may have.

In English Ecclesiastical Law no agreement or private determination is allowed to nullify a marriage, even though it involves the frustration of one of the principal ends of matrimony. English law looks to the consent as expressed, and will not allow the parties privately to derogate from their public professions. As Sir William Scott, later Lord Stowell, sitting as an ecclesiastical judge in a Church Court, laid down:

> It is in the intention of the parties that the substance of any contract subsists, and what is beyond or adverse to the intent does not belong to the

---

[1] See Esmein, op. cit., Vol. I, pp. 337–341. The doctrine appears to have survived the Reformation in England: see Swinburne, *Spousals*, Sect. XII, paras. 29 *et seq.*, pp. 134 *et seq.* (Swinburne's *Spousals*, although published in 1686, was written before 1621). The doctrine does not seem to have been applied to mere private reservations: see Swinburne, op. cit., Sect. XI, para. 13, p. 84; and therefore became obsolete when marriages were universally contracted by public rite in place of private agreement: see Sir William Scott's judgement in *Dalrymple* v. *Dalrymple*, cited p. 28 below.

[2] *The Greek Fathers*, 1908, p. 95.

contract. But then that intention is to be collected (primarily at least) from the words in which it is expressed; and in some systems of law, as in our own, it is pretty exclusively to be so collected. You are not to travel out of the intention expressed by the words to substitute an intention totally different and possibly inconsistent with the words ... [English law does not permit] of substituting another serious intention than that which the words express, to be proved by extrinsic evidence, and totally, as we phrase it, *dehors* the instrument. ... The parties are concluded to mean seriously, and deliberately, and intentionally, what they have avowed in the presence of God and man under all the sanctions of religion and law.[1]

So, in a subsequent case where the parties entered into a written agreement before marriage that they would never live together, the Court held that the condition was void as against public policy, that the marriage was valid and that a decree for restitution of conjugal rights should be pronounced.[2]

Conditional consent is sometimes described as a form of *error de qualitate*, and occurs where the presence or absence of some particular quality, e.g., virginity or freedom from disease, is stipulated by one of the parties as a *sine qua non* of the marriage. Doheny states that "to affect the matrimonial consent, the condition must have been placed at the time of the marriage or before the marriage and must not have been revoked."[3] It is obvious that the admission of such a practice as affecting the validity of marriages is extremely dangerous. The most strict judicial procedure can hardly prevent it from becoming an abuse, and it is not a sufficient answer to criticism to say that parties to such a proceeding can be punished in the *forum internum*. The objections to Defective Intention stated above also apply here, and the general adoption of such conditional consent as a ground for nullity in English law cannot be recommended.

It may, however, be suggested that some of the grounds for nullity introduced in 1937[4] are best understood and brought into conformity with traditional canonical principles if they are considered as falling under the head of conditional consent. Certain of them—concealed venereal disease, pregnancy, or recurrent fits of insanity or epilepsy—directly affect the matrimonial union, whether considered in terms of *copula carnalis* or of community of life in the wider sense. It would seem reasonable to see in these grounds a recognition by society of certain conditions which may be implicit in the

---

[1] *Dalrymple* v. *Dalrymple* (1811), 2 Hag. Con. 54, at pp. 105, 106; see also *Warrender* v. *Warrender* (1835), 2 Cl. and Fin. 488, at p. 530 *per* Lord Brougham.
[2] *Brodie* v. *Brodie*, [1917] P. 271.
[3] *Canonical Procedure in Matrimonial Cases*, Milwaukee, 1948, Vol. I, p. 943.
[4] See p. 23 above.

making of the marriage contract, so that a person who, within the space of one year from the date of the marriage, started proceedings for Nullity under one of these heads would be deemed to have made the absence of pregnancy, venereal disease, and recurrent fits of insanity or epilepsy a condition precedent to the marriage contract.[1]

4. *Conclusion*

We see no reason to criticize the present English Civil Law in regard to consent. We are opposed to any extension which could leave the validity of a marriage dependent upon the private stipulations or mental reservations of the parties.

[1] For an alternative way of regarding these grounds of nullity, namely as conditions annexed by law as terms of the marriage contract on the ground of public policy, see Chapter VI, p. 38 below.

CHAPTER V

SEXUAL CAPACITY AND CONSUMMATION

1. *Introductory*

ACCORDING TO some of the early canonists a marriage did not exist until it had been consummated, since until then the man and woman concerned had not become "one flesh".[1] The logical result, however, of the twelfth-century controversy which established consent as the essential element in marriage was to reduce the legal importance of the sexual act which followed the giving of that consent.[2] Therefore attention became focused on the quality and nature of consent. Consent was held to include consent to the *traditio corporum*; and, since its validity necessarily involved capacity, a marriage was regarded as valid if at the time that they gave their consent the man and woman were capable of consummating it. The actual sexual relations and the nature of the intercourse between man and wife were thenceforward of importance in any suit for Nullity in an English Court only in so far as they might help that Court to establish capacity or incapacity (impotence) at the time of the giving of consent.

2. *Meaning and Effect in English Civil Law*

The law of Nullity on the ground of impotence as administered in the English Courts to-day remains in principle that which was administered prior to 1858 in the English Ecclesiastical Courts.

Subject to approbation or "insincerity", a decree of Nullity may be granted at the suit of either partner to the marriage who can establish impotence at the date of the marriage which has persisted uncured and of which there is no reasonable prospect of cure.[3]

Impotence may be of two types:

(i) Organic—due to malformation or physical defect.

(ii) Psychological. This defect may render the subject impotent towards all possible partners, or may be purely relative, so that he or she is incapable

---

[1] Gen. 2. 24; Matt. 19. 5; Mark 10. 8.

[2] It must be added that in cases of papal dissolution of an unconsummated marriage the definition of consummation remained of the first importance, but such cases were infrequent before the sixteenth century, and did not affect the English Church after the Reformation.

[3] But for the exceptional case of aged persons, see Chapter III, p. 22, n. 4.

of intercourse with the other partner to the marriage, while yet capable of intercourse with some other person. Associated with this is the legal concept of "invincible repugnance" towards the other partner. This should be distinguished from "wilful refusal to consummate", since it is not due to a deliberate conscious act of the will but to deep-lying psychological causes.

The nature of the impotence which it is necessary to establish is inability to complete the act of intercourse. In defining the act of intercourse or consummation, Dr Lushington[1] in 1845 employed the canonists' phrase *vera copula* (true consummation), and on the facts of the particular case, in which the woman suffered from such malformation of the vagina as made complete penetration impracticable, granted a decree of Nullity.

Since this decision the invariable test applied by the English Courts in determining impotence has been the capacity of the man to effect complete penetration. It is important to emphasize that the English Ecclesiastical Courts never considered sterility or inability to conceive as constituting impotence.[2]

3. *Wilful Refusal to Consummate*

Before 1937 the English Courts had from time to time to consider marriage when one or other party had refused to attempt, or to allow the other to attempt, to consummate it. In such cases it was frequently inferred that the person so refusing was impotent,[3] but the Court was never driven off the ground that decrees of Nullity could only be made on proof of impotence or incapacity existing at the time of the marriage. Where, therefore, it was established that the refusal was "wilful", in the sense of a rational exercise of volition, and not the result of pathological disturbance, the refusal was not sufficient to justify a decree of Nullity on the ground of impotence.[4] The recommendation contained in the Report in 1912 of the Royal Commission on Divorce (paragraph 353), and supported also in the Minority Report, that wilful refusal should be a ground of nullity was founded on the view that such refusal indicated "unfitness to marry" undisclosed to the other party.

In 1937 Parliament introduced a new ground of nullity by enacting that, subject to certain provisos, a marriage should be voidable on the ground that it had "not been consummated owing to the wilful refusal of the respondent to consummate the marriage".[5]

1 *D.* v. *A.* (1845), 1 Rob. Ecc. 279.
2 Ibid., at p. 296.
3 *G.* v. *G.*, [1924] A. C. 349.
4 *Napier* v. *Napier*, [1915] P. 184.
5 Matrimonial Causes Act, 1937, s. 7 (1) (*a*), re-enacted in Matrimonial Causes Act 1950, s. 8 (1) (*a*). See Appendix 1, p. 49 below.

This provision represented a radical departure from the law as administered by the Ecclesiastical Courts, since it permitted a marriage to be annulled as a result of a subsequent event even though consent had been given by two persons capable of consummation. Thus on the strength of a post-nuptial event, a marriage valid when entered into could be treated as null and void.

The House of Lords, whilst declining to define the phrase "wilful refusal to consummate the marriage", has said that it connotes "a settled and definite decision come to without excuse".[1]

In applying this provision the Courts have had to consider the meaning of the word "consummation". In *Cowen* v. *Cowen*[2] the Court of Appeal, reversing the decision of the court of first instance,[3] held that a man who had consistently refused to have intercourse without a contraceptive had wilfully refused to consummate the marriage, since he had thereby prevented the procreation of children, described in the Prayer Book as one of the principal ends of marriage. In *Baxter* v. *Baxter*,[4] however, it was stated in the House of Lords that the procreation of children "does not appear to be a principal end of marriage as understood in Christendom".[5] It was held that the use of contraceptives does not preclude the consummation of the marriage, provided there has been full and complete penetration. Accordingly in Civil Law a marriage is held to have been consummated if it is proved that full penetration has been achieved. In the absence of "wilful refusal" it is therefore held valid if the parties were at the time of its celebration capable of effecting full penetration.[6]

4. *Roman Catholic Church*

The Roman Catholic Courts have given much attention to questions of nullity and to what constitutes consummation. The decisions of the Roman Catholic Courts establish three elements as essential to consummation[7], viz.:

(i) A sufficient erection of the male member.

(ii) Penetration by it into the vagina of the female.

(iii) The natural ejaculation of semen into the vagina.

Thus where *coitus interruptus* is practised or a contraceptive device is used by the male to prevent the entry of semen into the vagina, or where the male

1 *Horton* v. *Horton*, [1947] 2 All E. R. 871.
2 [1946] P. 36.
3 [1945] 2 All E. R. 197.
4 [1948] A. C. 274.
5 Ibid., at p. 286 *per* Lord Jowitt, L. C.
6 *R.* v. *R.*, [1952] 1 All E. R. 1194.
7 R. Naz, *Dictionnaire de Droit Canonique*, Vol. IV, cols. 362–87.

is unable to ejaculate, decrees of Nullity are granted; whereas when a woman used an occlusive pessary which would prevent conception, a decree would be refused.[1] The fact that a man may be sterile or that a woman may be incapable of conceiving are not grounds of nullity, although in one case the court did pronounce a decree when the semen of the man lacked spermatozoa.

The course of these decisions may be summarized by saying that the Roman Catholic Church regards a marriage as consummated when the male seed has been deposited in the vagina of the woman in the natural manner, irrespective of whether procreation has in fact followed.

5. *Church of England*

We hold that the true teaching of the Church in these matters is based on the ends of marriage as stated in the Book of Common Prayer and established by the English Ecclesiastical Courts: that is, that the consent given in marriage involves consent to consummate the marriage and the capacity to do so.

If the parties are at the time of the marriage incapable of *vera copula* or a true conjunction, in the sense that they are unable to perform the act of intercourse in the natural manner, the marriage may be annulled.[2] We accept that the act to be performed must be that which may, in Nature, result in the procreation of children, although for one reason or another it may not so result in any particular case. That act, as we understand it, involves penetration by the erect member of the man into the vagina of the woman so that ejaculation may there take place.

6. *The Problems*

In the light of the above we have carefully reviewed the law relating to consummation as administered in the Civil Courts. It is apparent that the following difficulties arise:

(i) Can the Church agree with the statement made in the House of Lords that the procreation of children does not appear to be a principal end of marriage as understood in Christendom?

Whilst the Church of England has never regarded sterility as a ground of nullity, we cannot accept this statement: it is in direct conflict with the Book of Common Prayer, and, as we think, went beyond what was necessary to

---

1 Ibid., cols. 362–3.
2 For the question of artificial insemination see p. 35 and Chapter VI, p. 39.

4

the decision of the Court.[1] Further, Lord Jowitt justified his dictum as follows: "Nor does it [the procreation of children] appear to be a principal end of marriage as understood in Christendom, which, as Lord Penzance said in *Hyde* v. *Hyde*, 'may *for this purpose*[2] be defined as the voluntary union for life of one man and one woman, to the exclusion of all others'":[3] but Lord Penzance's "purpose" had nothing to do with procreation of children, but only with the effect to be given to polygamous marriages. Finally, the dictum contradicts a wealth of previous judicial authority which the House of Lords did not review.[4]

(ii) Can "wilful refusal to consummate" be accepted as a true ground of nullity?

We cannot find any logic in a provision by which a marriage, valid at the time it was made, can be declared void *ab initio* as a result of a subsequent event. In very many cases where a partner refuses to consummate a marriage refusal is due to some psychological incapacity, and such cases can be effectively dealt with as cases of impotence, refusal being treated as evidence of incapacity, as it was before 1937. We recognize also that there are cases[5] where two persons who are capable go through a ceremony of marriage and then part. Such cases occasionally arise when previous intercourse has taken place, and it is desired to legitimize the child, although one or other or both parties have no intention of setting up home together. Such cases can properly be dealt with as cases of desertion.

(iii) Can the Church accept penetration as a satisfactory test of consummation or capacity?

It must be recognized that the present Civil Law has affirmed marriages which many would regard as unnatural, and has in a few cases permitted the annulment of others even though children have been born in wedlock.

---

[1] A judicial pronouncement extraneous to and unnecessary for the decision is termed *obiter dictum*, and does not constitute binding law.

[2] Our italics.

[3] *Baxter* v. *Baxter*, [1948] A. C. 274, at p. 286.

[4] E.g., "The primary and most legitimate object of wedlock—the procreation of children": *Brown* v. *Brown* (1828), 1 Hag. Ecc. 523, at p. 524 *per* Sir John Nicholl.

"Neither of two principal ends of matrimony can be attained, namely a lawful indulgence of the passions to prevent licentiousness, and the procreation of children": *D.* v. *A.* (1845), 1 Rob. Ecc. 279, at p. 298 *per* Dr Lushington.

"The procreation of children being the main object of marriage, the contract contains by implication, as an essential term, the capacity for consummation": *G.* v. *M.* (1885), 10 App. Cas. 171, at p. 204 *per* Lord Fitzgerald.

See also Ayliffe, *Parergon Juris Canonici*, 1726, p. 360, tit. "Of Marriage"; Oughton, *Ordo Judiciorum*, 1728, tit. 193, par. 17.

[5] Cf. *Napier* v. *Napier*, [1915] P. 184.

Thus in Civil Law a marriage is valid, and a decree of Nullity will be refused, provided penetration can be established, even though

(a) the man is incapable of ejaculation[1],

(b) a contraceptive device has been used to prevent contact between the organ of the man and that of the woman and the emission of semen into the vagina,[2] or

(c) the man has practised *coitus interruptus*.[3]

On the other hand decrees of Nullity have been granted where a woman has borne a child

(a) after incomplete intercourse with her husband, and as a result of *fecundatio ab extra*,[4] or

(b) as a result of artificial insemination with the semen of her husband, but where he had proved incapable of attaining the necessary erection to effect penetration.[5]

After hearing the evidence of medical experts we are satisfied that the only test which can be applied in law is that of penetration. Degrees of ejaculation may occur during intercourse which may be imperceptible to either party, and could only be detected by medical examination immediately thereafter; whilst the quality of fluid issuing from the male is also impossible to ascertain without medical examination in circumstances which are impracticable. We consider that evidence of such a character can seldom be available.

Whilst, therefore, we cannot regard penetration as a complete description of consummation or *vera copula*, we feel bound to accept it as the only practical test.

We regard it as mistaken to seek to distinguish between types of contraceptives. To suggest that if one type is employed a marriage is consummated, but that if another is used it is not, seems to us to involve absurd distinctions; whilst evidence of the condition or effectiveness of the particular article used would involve Courts in inquiries which would be quite impossible to resolve.

We have been particularly concerned at the decisions by which nullity has been decreed despite the birth of a child to a partner after artificial insemination or *fecundatio ab extra*. It does not appear that the Courts, in granting such decrees, gave sufficient weight to the doctrine of approbation, whereby

---

1 *R.* v. *R.*, [1952] 1 All E. R. 1194.
2 *Baxter* v. *Baxter*, [1948] A. C. 274.
3 *White* v. *White*, [1948] P. 230; *Cackett* v. *Cackett*, [1950] P. 253.
4 *Clarke* v. *Clarke*, [1943] 2 All E. R. 540.
5 *R.E.L.* v. *E.L.*, [1949] P. 211.

a partner may, in certain circumstances, be precluded from disputing the validity of the marriage.[1] In view of a recent decision,[2] where a husband was not permitted to impeach the validity of his marriage after he and his wife had adopted a child, we think it reasonable to expect that where a child has been born as a result of the act or consent of both parties, a decree of Nullity may, in future, be refused on the ground that the marriage has been approbated.

[1] See Chapter III, p. 20 above.
[2] *W.* v. *W.*, [1952] P. 152; but cf. *Slater* v. *Slater*, [1953] P. 235.

CHAPTER VI

CHURCH AND STATE

1. *General*

HOW FAR is it right or valuable for the Church to have a different law from the State? It is, of course, clear that unless one completely identifies the ecclesiastical with the civil organization, there is almost bound to be some difference between the two. But there are many disadvantages in having two standards or systems of law in one country, and they become especially acute when Church and State are so closely connected as they are in England. The Civil Law with all its elaborate machinery can be used to ascertain facts and thus reach decisions which could not be ascertained or reached with the same certainty by any organization which was less completely equipped; and for this reason public opinion will more readily recognize the justice of a decision given in the secular Courts.

The Church is, however, a theocracy, and the law by which it lives is founded upon divine revelation. If it is satisfied that the law of the State is not in agreement with that revelation, then the Church must abide by its own law.

This does not necessarily mean that there must be an internecine conflict. The Church must recognize that there are some members of the State who do not accept Christian standards of marriage. For them laws of Marriage enacted by the State will suffice. The Church must, however, say that in addition it is compelled to impose a stricter discipline upon its own members, and to call upon Christian people to adopt a more rigourist attitude. Thus in 1938 the Convocations of Canterbury and York stated that "the Church of England is competent to enact such a discipline of its own in regard to marriage as may from time to time appear most salutary and efficacious."[1] This in point of fact is what the Church has done in regard to the law of Divorce. It recognizes that the State declares marriages dissolved and allows those who have been released from the marriage tie to marry again, even though the partner of the first marriage is still alive. But on behalf of its own members the Church has said by resolution of the Convocations that in such cases the marriage service should not be used.[2]

[1] Resolution 4 of June 1938. See *Acts of the Convocations of Canterbury and York*, ed. Smethurst and Wilson, S.P.C.K., 1948, p. 91.

[2] See Resolution 3 of June 1938, op. cit. A parallel case is envisaged by the proposed amendment to Draft Canon XXXVIII quoted on p. viii of this Report.

It is also the duty of the Church from time to time to suggest to the State amendments of the marriage laws; and if these suggestions are rejected, the Church may have to ask its own members to act in the spirit of those amendments, even though they were not accepted by the State. In accordance with its terms of reference, therefore, the Commission has been bound to consider:

(i) whether it should suggest any modifications in the existing civil marriage law of England in regard to nullity, and

(ii) whether it should recommend the setting up of special Church Courts or the use of other ecclesiastical machinery to deal with matters relating to nullity which fall outside the provision of the present Civil Law.

2. Conclusions on the present Civil Law of Nullity

(i) The 1937 grounds for nullity

(a) *Wilful refusal.* We can only regard this provision as repugnant to the logic which has always governed the law of Nullity in Canon and Civil Law. We do not see how a marriage admittedly valid at the time of celebration can properly be treated as void *ab initio* on the ground of a subsequent event. In the light of the decision in *Baxter* v. *Baxter*,[1] with which we agree (albeit not with all the terms in which it was expressed), this type of case now appears to be limited in practice mainly to cases of refusal which in reality spring from psychological incapacity, and to those rare cases where marriage has been contracted from some ulterior motive with no intention that cohabitation should follow. The former type can properly and logically be dealt with in accordance with the law relating to impotence, whilst the latter should be dealt with otherwise than by annulment. Once the principle that a subsequent event can be a ground for nullity is accepted, the essential difference between nullity and divorce disappears.

(b) *The other grounds.* We have already suggested[2] that these grounds can be accepted as an application of the doctrine of conditional consent. An alternative way is to regard them as terms of the marriage contract implied by law on grounds of public policy, just as the law implies a term that each party is capable of sexual intercourse.[3] This would approximate to the canonical impediment *honestas publica.*

---

[1] [1948] A. C. 274.

[2] P. 28 above.

[3] See G. v. M. (1885), 10 App. Cas. 171, at p. 204 *per* Lord Fitzgerald, cited on p. 22 above. Lord Merrivale in *Mitford* v. *Mitford*, [1923] P. 130, at p. 131, suggested that a statutory enactment in the Prussian Code, providing a ground for rendering a marriage voidable, was to be regarded as a condition annexed by law to the marriage contract.

We therefore consider that the grounds for nullity set out in Section 7 (1) of the Matrimonial Causes Act, 1937,[1] other than "wilful refusal to consummate", can be accepted by the Church.

We should, however, mention that medical witnesses suggested that the ground of nullity by reason of recurrent fits of epilepsy was too widely drawn. They pointed out that there are many different sorts of epilepsy, some permanently suppressed, which could not be thought to affect the matrimonial consent or *consortium*, more than many other inherent maladies. We think that this objection is based on a misapprehension: the Statute refers to "recurrent *fits* of epilepsy", and not to epilepsy in general.

(ii) *Nullity despite the birth of a child*

As already stated,[2] we are concerned at the way in which decrees of Nullity have been granted on proof of incapacity to penetrate notwithstanding the fact that a child has been born as a result of imperfect intercourse[3] or of artificial insemination with the seed of the husband.[4] (A similar problem would arise in the case of artificial insemination with the seed of some other man but with the husband's consent.) We believe that these decisions have been given as a result of a failure to raise or apply the doctrine of approbation, which has been restated in a more recent case.[5] Whether this is the right explanation or not, we do not think that annulment should be permitted on grounds of impotence where a child has resulted from the joint act or with the mutual consent of both parties. We are aware that in cases where the Court considers that an important question of law is raised the Queen's Proctor is invited to attend and assist the Court with legal argument. The importance of this practice, which is comparable to the function of the *defensor vinculi* in the Courts of the Roman Catholic Church, is obvious in cases where the petition is otherwise unopposed, and we would urge that it be adopted in all cases of Nullity on grounds of impotence where a child has been born in wedlock. We suggest that these matters be raised with the Royal Commission now sitting, with a view to ensuring the application of the doctrine of approbation.

(iii) *Suggested additional grounds for nullity*

Suggestions have been made to us for extending the grounds of nullity to include impotence due to vasectomy after marriage, and also the discovery

1 Now Matrimonial Causes Act, 1950, Section 8 (1).
2 See Chapter V, Section 6.
3 *Clarke* v. *Clarke*, [1943] 2 All E. R. 540.
4 *R.E.L.* v. *E.L.*, [1949] P. 211.
5 *W.* v. *W.*, [1952] P. 152; but cf. *Slater* v. *Slater*, [1953] P. 235. See Chapter V, p. 35 above.

after marriage of the presence of such a *Rhesus factor*[1] as would render unlikely the production of children who would survive. We are of opinion that neither of these grounds could properly be made the basis for a decree of Nullity. The former we reject because it is *ex causa subsequenti*. As for the latter, sterility (which involves inability to produce children at all) was not a ground for nullity in Canon Law, and is not in English Civil Law, and *a fortiori* the fact that children are unlikely to survive cannot be a ground for nullity.

We have considered a suggestion that homosexuality in certain cases might be a ground for nullity. The term homosexuality is often used inaccurately or vaguely. Although it is frequently regarded as a male phenomenon, it is hardly less extensive among women than among men. Confusion also arises between (*a*) the *condition* of sexual inversion in men and women, the real cause of which is still not definitely known, and the cure at best uncertain, if not, in most cases, impossible; and (*b*) the commission of homosexual *acts* which may be due either to inversion or to perversion. The true invert is really a sick man or woman, psychologically diseased. The pervert is usually a degenerate or vicious heterosexual who, for one reason or another, has taken to indulgence in homosexual acts.

The question is whether inversion or perversion fall to be considered under one of the existing dirimentary impediments recognized by the Civil Law or by the law of the Church and ought to constitute a new ground for nullity.

There is no precedent for treating perversion as a diriment impediment to marriage, and there would be the gravest objections to its becoming one. In the case of true inversion some claim that there is reasonable cause for making it a ground for nullity, and specially so when, although antecedent to the marriage, it is wilfully concealed. We are assured that there are many factors involved on which there can be divergence of medical and psychological opinion. The whole question needs to be examined in the light of further knowledge and experience before any recommendation can be made to effect a change of the law. We are informed that the subject is to be reviewed by a working group of the Church of England Moral Welfare Council.[2]

One aspect of the matter needs to be brought to the attention of those who

---

[1] Modern medical research has shown that 85% of human beings have blood which is "Rhesus positive" and 15% have blood which is "Rhesus negative". When the father's blood is "Rhesus positive" and the mother's "Rhesus negative", the mother's blood forms antibodies to the paternal Rhesus factors in the new-born child, which destroy the red cells in the child's blood. As a consequence the new-born infant is liable to die of anaemia at birth (Haemolytic Disease of the New-born). It should be emphasized, however, that this only happens in about 1 in 40 of such marriages. Recent research has also materially reduced the mortality of infants from this cause.

[2] Since our Report was signed, the Report of this Group has been published.

urge inverts to be married, with an assurance that marital experience will effectively cure the abnormality. In some cases the inversion may remain as fixed as before, and there may be no hope of satisfactory married life. Very serious thought ought to be given, and the best possible medical opinion obtained, before urging such a step. We sympathize with both partners to such a marriage where no cure has been effected. At the same time we cannot recommend that inversion should become a ground for nullity.[1]

Another factor which, it has been suggested to us, the Church might recognize as a ground for nullity is Defective Intention. This is fully considered in Chapter IV of our Report and we reject it for the reasons there stated.

3. *Suggestions for the Reform of Canon Law*

(i) *Ecclesiastical Courts*

We have given careful consideration to the advisability of setting up some machinery by which the Church could review decisions made in the secular Courts, in order to see whether they should be accepted in the exercise of ecclesiastical discipline. It will be remembered that the draft Canon XXXVI, Clause 2,[2] envisaged the possibility of a couple obtaining a divorce when they might perhaps have obtained a decree of Nullity. If one of them later asks to be allowed to contract a new marriage in church, and credibly asserts that the previous marriage was in truth a nullity, ought the bishop to regard himself as bound by the decision of the secular Court and refuse the request? If not there seem to be two possible courses:

(*a*) *To set up Ecclesiastical Courts to review all the evidence and, if necessary, examine witnesses to decide whether a plea of Nullity could have been maintained.* If these courts are to deal satisfactorily with questions of nullity they must have powers comparable to those possessed by the secular Courts when determining similar issues: in particular they would require power to compel the attendance of, and answers by, witnesses. It is most unlikely that such powers would be granted by the State. So long as the Church remains established it would be highly anomalous to have two sets of Courts with power to administer law on the same topics. The State could hardly contemplate the confusion which would result were the same marriage declared dissolved by one Court and annulled by another. In the absence of these powers a Church Court might be denied vital evidence and its procedure stultified. The evidence of a party who has affirmed the validity of a marriage

---

1 Inversion of a homosexual nature may cause permanent and incurable impotence in a heterosexual union: such impotence at the time of the marriage is an existing ground of nullity.

2 See p. vii of the Introduction.

in order to obtain a decree of Dissolution should be subject to close scrutiny when he or she asserts that the marriage was not in fact valid at all.

The organization of such Courts might present a formidable administrative problem. They would constitute a major expense if they were to be staffed by trained lawyers and adequate facilities were to be provided for poor litigants. It is impossible to assess even approximately the number of genuine cases of the type referred to above, and in the absence of such evidence it would be difficult to justify the organization and expenditure involved. Failure to conduct such Courts with efficiency and impartiality might bring grave discredit on the Church, and we do not consider their establishment warranted in present circumstances.

(b) *To allow the bishop, taking such legal advice as he may desire, to decide whether the proposed marriage shall take place in church or not.* Already, the bishop in the exercise of his pastoral office is often called upon to decide as to the re-admission to Holy Communion of those who have re-married after divorce.[1] It is urged, therefore, that to decide whether or no a marriage that has been dissolved was in fact void is a natural extension of his pastoral administration. There are, however, grave objections to such a procedure:

1. Unlike re-admission to Holy Communion after divorce, the question of nullity is not a pastoral issue. It is a weighty question of fact and law of a highly complex nature, which demands expert and experienced judgement, and cannot be handled in any amateur fashion. Canon 106 of 1603/4 lays down the principle that "no sentence shall be given . . . for annulling of pretended Matrimony, but in open Court, and in the seat of Justice."

2. Experience both in Civil and Ecclesiastical Courts has shown that a true judgement, in a case of Nullity, can seldom rest upon the unsupported testimony of the parties themselves, even when given in good faith. Canon 105 of 1603/4 insists on the need of additional evidence and proof:

> Forasmuch as matrimonial causes have been always reckoned and reputed amongst the weightiest, and therefore require the greater caution, when they come to be handled and debated in judgement, especially in causes wherein Matrimony, having been in the Church duly solemnized, is required upon any suggestion or pretext whatsoever to be dissolved or annulled; We do straitly charge and enjoin, that in all proceedings to Divorce and Nullities of Matrimony, good circumspection and advice be used, and that the truth may (as far as possible) be sifted out by the

---

[1] Cf. Lambeth Conference 1948: Resolution 96. For the Convocation resolutions arising from this, see *Acts of the Convocations of Canterbury and York*, S.P.C.K., 1948, p. 91–4.

deposition of witnesses, and other lawful proofs and evictions, and that credit be not given to the sole confession of the parties themselves, howsoever taken upon oath, either within or without the Court.

A bishop, however, would have no legal authority to summon witnesses or to call for documents. Furthermore, in this matter of evidence, we are informed that the great majority of cases where a petition for Divorce is preferred to one for Nullity are those where impotence is concerned. The petitioner has perhaps shrunk from the medical examination involved and the recital of intimate details even *in camera*, or has sought to avoid the possible stigma of incapacity. But the overwhelming testimony before us established that it was not safe to dispense with a medical examination in deciding on the question of impotence, nor to rely solely on the statement of the petitioner, even when given in good faith.

3. A decree of Divorce presumes that the marriage has been valid. An appeal to the bishop to regard it as null and void might be dealt with in one of two ways, either formally or informally. In the latter case the bishop, either in his own pastoral dealings with the applicant or through the clergy in close touch with the case, would satisfy himself as to the applicant's good faith and then act accordingly. This, however, would mean adopting a line of action completely at variance with the canons above quoted, and to the majority of us at least the question of nullity seems far too important to be dealt with in so informal a manner. If, on the other hand, the case were dealt with formally, the reconsideration of such a decision of the Civil Court by a bishop would demand his acting upon a uniform standard of judgement based upon an elaborate code of principles. This could hardly obtain where forty-three diocesan bishops would be dealing, independently, with the difficult problems of nullity, however carefully and conscientiously they sought to discharge their duty. Even if the bishop associated with himself the chancellor of the diocese, or called in other help, this could only result, in effect, in setting up forty-three unofficial Courts in place of the Church Courts the establishment of which we have discussed and rejected.

As a modification of the above proposal, it was suggested that a panel of advisers, appointed by the bishops and accepted throughout the province, should be established, and that the bishop should refer cases to this panel for their advice and accept the opinion offered to him by this panel. The panel would not pronounce a decree of Nullity, but would investigate, in accordance with a system of rules to be formulated by the Convocations, whether there was any reason that a spouse whose marriage had been dissolved might marry a second time in church. On the other hand, it was pointed out that the issue would still remain a judicial, not a pastoral, responsibility, demanding correct judicial procedure; and permission to marry another person in church would be tantamount to the pronouncement of a decree of Nullity. The reasons for the decision of the panel of advisers would inevitably be demanded, and in some cases challenged; and an escape behind a wall of silence would invite suspicion and hostility. In effect the panel of advisers would be an unofficial Church Court, with its limitations increased and deprived of its advantages.

These considerations led us to the conclusion that if there were to be any appeal from the pronouncement of a Divorce in the Civil Courts, it could only be to some central Ecclesiastical Court such as we have already ruled out.

By far the most satisfactory solution is to take steps to prevent, as far as possible, a petitioner who has grounds for a decree of Nullity from seeking the alternative of Divorce, either through ignorance or for reasons of expediency. If an approach was made to the General Council of the Bar and the Law Society, and it was pointed out that a decree of Divorce instead of Nullity debarred the parties concerned from a future marriage in church, much could be done, especially in Legal Aid cases, to impress upon counsel and solicitors the desirability of advising their clients to apply for a decree of Nullity where possible. It is, also, the responsibility of the Church to see that the general public appreciate the importance of the distinction between nullity and divorce.

(ii) *Proposed new Clause in Draft Canon XXXVIII forbidding the re-marriage in church of those who have obtained a decree on grounds of wilful refusal*

In connection with the inclusion of "wilful refusal to consummate" as one of the new grounds for nullity laid down in the 1937 Act, the Commission was requested to consider the amendment to Canon XXXVIII of the draft revised Canons of which notice was given in Canterbury Convocation by the late Bishop of Oxford.[1] The purpose of this amendment was to forbid the subsequent marriage in church to another of any person who had obtained a decree of Nullity on the ground of wilful refusal to consummate.

We have already indicated that we favour the retention of refusal to consummate as a ground for nullity where it results from psychological incapacity, such refusal being necessarily in contra-distinction to "wilful" refusal. If refusal to consummate were treated as evidence of incapacity (as in proper cases we think it should be), the decree of Nullity in such cases would be given on the ground of impotence, and would be open to no canonical objection. In that case the suggested amendment would be unnecessary.

1 See p. viii of the Introduction.

Unless and until such revision takes place we must regard *wilful* refusal to consummate as an unsatisfactory ground for nullity.

Nonetheless we doubt the wisdom of making the proposed amendment to Canon XXXVIII at the present time. It should be borne in mind that the Convocation of York and the Upper House of the Convocation of Canterbury formally accepted in 1937/38 all the new grounds of nullity laid down in the 1937 Act, including the ground of wilful refusal. On the other hand, the Lower House of the Convocation of Canterbury refused to approve them without further consideration, and on 28 May 1937 passed the following Resolution:

> That serious consideration should be given to the question of the desirability of amending the present law of nullity, and that His Grace the President be humbly requested to appoint a Committee, consisting of persons skilled in theology, canon and civil law, and medical science, to consider the law of nullity.[1]

It was in fact this very Resolution which in the first place led up to the appointment of the present Commission.

Thus, while it cannot be said that the Church of England as a whole has through its Convocations accepted "wilful refusal" as a valid ground for nullity, the action of three of the four Houses of the Convocations and the general practice of the Church since that time may have created the impression that the Church has accepted it. Since 1937 persons who have obtained decrees of Nullity on this ground have been married again in Church without objection, and it might be regarded as unfair to forbid the same right to those who might obtain similar decrees after 1955. We would therefore suggest that any amendment of Canon XXXVIII on the lines proposed should be deferred until the Royal Commission has reported and it has been seen whether Section 8 (1) (*a*) of the Matrimonial Causes Act, 1950, is to be amended.

(iii) *Suggested new canon on nullity*

It seems desirable that a new canon should embody so much of the additions to the law of Nullity introduced by the Matrimonial Causes Act, 1937, as is acceptable to the Church. Precedent for such a canon is to be found in the amendments of Canons 62 and 99 of 1603.

The first of these two canons deals, among other things, with the hours between which marriages may be solemnized. The canon was amended in 1887 to extend the hours and also to make it unnecessary that matrimony should take place in the time of Divine Service. It has still more recently

[1] See *Chronicle of Convocation* for May, 1937, pp. xix, 427–35.

been amended to extend the hours for marriage further, following a similar statutory extension. Canon 99 concerns the Table of Kindred and Affinity, and was amended in 1946 in such wise as to make plain the Church's acceptance of certain statutory alterations in the Prohibited Degrees. We include among our Recommendations a suggestion that consideration be given to incorporating the findings of the Commission in the Canon Law of the Church of England.

CHAPTER VII

CONCLUSIONS AND RECOMMENDATIONS

1. Both Church and State agree that marriage is the voluntary union for life of one man and one woman to the exclusion of all others. Although the Church recognizes marriages contracted after divorce by the Civil Courts as legally binding, it makes a distinction between legal and canonical marriages and exercises its own discipline over its own members in either case.

2. The three-fold purpose of marriage is:
   (a) the procreation of children, to be brought up in the fear and nurture of the Lord;
   (b) the hallowing and directing aright of the natural instincts and affections;
   (c) the mutual society, help, and comfort that the one ought to have of the other.

The Commission rejects the contention that the procreation of children is not a principal end of marriage.

3. No marriage is valid unless mutual consent has been freely given and received. Where such consent has been expressed in the proper form no previous agreement to frustrate any part of its purpose, no mental reservation on the part of either partner as to the fulfilment of its obligations, and no subsequent event can invalidate the marriage.

4. The Commission is satisfied that ability to effect or permit penetration must be accepted as the practical test of sexual capacity.

5. We recommend that the doctrine of approbation should be invoked whenever a child has resulted from the joint act, or with the consent, of both parties (e.g., by artificial insemination or legal adoption), and that in such cases the marriage should not be voidable even though the legal test of capacity has not been satisfied. We suggest that this recommendation and the discussion on p. 39, Chapter VI, be transmitted to the Royal Commission on Divorce with a view to necessary action by the State.

6. The Commission considers that, with the exception of wilful refusal to consummate, the additional grounds for nullity introduced by Parliament in 1937 (now contained in the Matrimonial Causes Act, 1950, s. 8) may be

accepted, and recommends that consideration be given to incorporating its findings in the Canon Law of the Church of England.

7. The Commission cannot accept "wilful refusal to consummate" as a satisfactory ground for nullity, and recommends that the following alteration in the law be proposed to the Royal Commission:

1. Sub-section (1) (a) of Section 8 of the Matrimonial Causes Act, 1950, is hereby repealed.

2. The following sub-section shall be added to Section 8 of the Matrimonial Causes Act, 1950:

   "(3) In any proceedings for Nullity of Marriage, the Court may draw an inference of sexual incapacity at the time of the marriage from evidence that the marriage has not been consummated owing to the refusal of the Respondent to consummate the marriage."

We believe this proposed addition to be declaratory of the law as it stands.

In default of some such alteration within a reasonable time, we recommend that Convocation should accept the amendment proposed to Draft Canon XXXVIII and discussed on pp. 44 ff. above.

8. The Commission recommends that in any case where a person has obtained a decree of Divorce in a secular Court and it is subsequently suggested that a decree of Nullity might have been obtained, the Church should nevertheless accept the decree of the Civil Court as decisive. With a view to the avoidance of such cases the assistance of the legal profession should be enlisted.

9. The Commission does not, at any rate at the present time, recommend the establishment of Church Courts to deal with cases of alleged Nullity, and considers that the use of any less formal machinery would be undesirable.

SIGNATURES TO THE REPORT

†WM: LONDIN: (*Chairman*)

†WILFRED BLACKBURN	CHRISTOPHER ROFFEN:	†KENNETH OXON:
ERIC KEMP	NORMAN PLYMOUTH	L. LEONARD KNIGHTALL
F. E. P. S. LANGTON	WM: LATEY	NOEL MIDDLETON
H. J. PHILLIMORE	A. S. PICTON	EDWARD C. RATCLIFF

J. E. S. SIMON   R. A. TALBOT

A. F. SMETHURST (*Secretary*)

RECENT STATUTORY PROVISIONS RELATING TO THE LAW OF NULLITY

MATRIMONIAL CAUSES ACT, 1950

Additional grounds for decrees of Nullity

8.—(1) In addition to any other grounds on which a marriage is by law void or voidable, a marriage shall be voidable on the ground

(a) that the marriage has not been consummated owing to the wilful refusal of the respondent to consummate the marriage; or

(b) that either party to the marriage was at the time of the marriage of unsound mind or a mental defective within the meaning of the Mental Deficiency Acts, 1913 to 1938, or subject to recurrent fits of insanity or epilepsy; or

(c) that the respondent was at the time of the marriage suffering from venereal disease in a communicable form; or

(d) that the respondent was at the time of the marriage pregnant by some person other than the petitioner:

Provided that, in the cases specified in paragraphs (b), (c), and (d) of this sub-section, the Court shall not grant a decree unless it is satisfied

(i) that the petitioner was at the time of the marriage ignorant of the facts alleged;

(ii) that proceedings were instituted within a year from the date of the marriage; and

(iii) that marital intercourse with the consent of the petitioner has not taken place since the discovery by the petitioner of the existence of the grounds for a decree.

(2) Nothing in this section shall be construed as validating any marriage which is by law void, but with respect to which a decree of Nullity has not been granted.

MARRIAGE ACT, 1949

Part I. Restrictions on Marriage

1.—(1) A marriage solemnized between a man and any of the persons mentioned in the first column of Part I of the First Schedule to this Act, or between a woman and any of the persons mentioned in the second column of the said Part I, shall be void.

(2) A marriage solemnized between a man and any of the persons mentioned in the first column of Part II of the said First Schedule, or between a woman and any of the persons mentioned in the second column of the said Part II, shall not be void or voidable by reason only of affinity.

(3) A marriage which by virtue of the last foregoing sub-section is not void or voidable if solemnized after the decease of any person shall be void if solemnized during the lifetime of that person.

2.—A marriage solemnized between persons either of whom is under the age of sixteen shall be void.

3.—(1) Where the marriage of an infant, not being a widower or widow, is intended to be solemnized on the authority of a certificate issued by a superintendent registrar under Part III of this Act, whether by licence or without licence, the consent of the person or persons specified in the Second Schedule to this Act shall be required. . . .

(4) A clergyman shall not be liable to ecclesiastical censure for solemnizing the marriage of an infant after the publication of banns without the consent of the parents or guardians of the infant unless he had notice of the dissent of any person who is entitled to give notice of dissent under the last foregoing sub-section. . . .

The First Schedule
KINDRED AND AFFINITY

PART I
Prohibited degrees of relationship

Mother	Father
Daughter	Son
Father's mother	Father's father
Mother's mother	Mother's father
Son's daughter	Son's son
Daughter's daughter	Daughter's son
Sister	Brother
Wife's mother	Husband's father
Wife's daughter	Husband's son
Father's wife	Mother's husband
Son's wife	Daughter's husband
Father's father's wife	Father's mother's husband
Mother's father's wife	Mother's mother's husband
Wife's father's mother	Husband's father's father
Wife's mother's mother	Husband's mother's father
Wife's son's daughter	Husband's son's son
Wife's daughter's daughter	Husband's daughter's son
Son's son's wife	Son's daughter's husband
Daughter's son's wife	Daughter's daughter's husband
Father's sister	Father's brother
Mother's sister	Mother's brother
Brother's daughter	Brother's son
Sister's daughter	Sister's son

PART II
Statutory exceptions from prohibited degrees of relationship

Deceased wife's sister	Deceased sister's husband
Deceased brother's wife	Deceased husband's brother
Deceased wife's brother's daughter	Father's deceased sister's husband
Deceased wife's sister's daughter	Mother's deceased sister's husband
Father's deceased brother's wife	Deceased husband's brother's son
Mother's deceased brother's wife	Deceased husband's sister's son
Deceased wife's father's sister	Brother's deceased daughter's husband
Deceased wife's mother's sister	Sister's deceased daughter's husband
Brother's deceased son's wife	Deceased husband's father's brother
Sister's deceased son's wife	Deceased husband's mother's brother

Note: In Section 79 (1) of this Act (Interpretation) the following definitions are included, with reference to the above Schedule:

"brother" includes a brother of the half-blood;

"sister" includes a sister of the half-blood.

APPENDIX 2

STATISTICS OF NULLITY SUITS

IT HAS been found impossible to obtain an analysis of suits for Nullity arising in Provincial centres, but the attached analysis relating to petitions for Nullity filed in London shows the figures of the various grounds for nullity alleged in those filed in London.

It has also been ascertained from the Annual Abstract of Statistics for England (and Wales) for the years 1942 to 1948 inclusive that the number of suits for Nullity filed has been as follows:

	Husbands	Wives
Cases filed in London	2,539	1,672
Cases filed in Provinces	1,187	686

This gives a total of 6,084 suits for Nullity throughout England and Wales during seven years, i.e., an average of 869. The proportion of petitions by husbands to petitions by wives varies only slightly as between London and Provincial cases, and it is considered reasonable to suppose that if the Provincial cases were analysed as in the attached table the proportions would be approximately the same as they are for London cases.

It will be understood that for various reasons, e.g., abandonment of the suit, failure of evidence, dismissal of the petition, a proportion of these cases has not resulted in decrees of Nullity, but direct information is not available.

Referring to the table of analysis it will be seen that Incapacity and Invalidity (e.g., bigamy, lack of form, duress, etc.) are not distinguished, but the cases of Invalidity are almost negligible in number: a notional average of 10 cases of Invalidity per annum would probably exceed the actual average.

Again, taking the table for the years 1942 to 1948 inclusive, the analysis shows that out of a total of 4,211 cases in London, averaging 601 per annum, petitions filed in London on the ground of Incapacity (including Invalidity) numbered 2,365, averaging 338 per annum, and those filed in London on the ground of Wilful Refusal numbered 1,611, averaging 230 per annum: a total of 3,976 together, giving an average of 568 per annum: in rough proportions of nearly three cases of Incapacity to two cases of Wilful Refusal.

There can be no doubt that war-time conditions aggravated the evil of hasty and ill-considered marriages; the aggravation is especially marked in suits based on the ground afforded by Sect. 7 (1) (d) of the Matrimonial Causes Act, 1937 (pregnancy by another man): and another cause of the increase in suits on the ground of Wilful Refusal can be traced to the unfortunate decision of the Court of Appeal in the case of Cowen v. Cowen, with which the House of Lords has since disagreed in the case of Baxter v. Baxter, but which temporarily left it open to suitors to claim decrees of Nullity on the ground that marital intercourse with contraceptives does not amount to consummation of marriage. For some time, too, there was doubt whether *coitus interruptus* amounted to non-consummation.

Total of Decrees Nisi pronounced
(Taken from the official Abstract of Statistics)

Year	Divorce	Nullity
1938	7,621	170
1939	7,019	178
1940	7,111	139
1941	6,318	143
1942	8,608	230
1943	10,724	330
1944	14,356	406
1945	18,982	500
1946	31,871	861
1947	52,249	1,543
1948	40,764	894
1949	33,967	654
1950	29,482	584
1951	29,936	559
1952	31,966	655
1953	29,275	596

These figures are for decrees *nisi* pronounced in England and Wales only.
The *preliminary* figures for 1949 have been split up for illustration, as follows:

	Dissolution	Nullity
London	14,468	363
Provinces	19,747	301
	34,215	664

It will, however, be understood that this illustration is no criterion of the proportion of cases heard in London and of those heard in the Provinces in earlier years, as the facilities for cases to be dealt with in the Provinces have been greatly increased in recent years.
The total figures of all decrees *nisi* granted *in London only* for 1950–2 are as follows:

	Dissolution	Nullity
1950	11,897	297
1951	11,974	290
1952	11,669	333

NULLITY PETITIONS FILED IN LONDON

	Year	Incapacity or Invalidity	Wilful Refusal	Lunacy	Pregnancy	Venereal	Total	
1942	Husband	109	103	—	17	—	229	
	Wife	98	32	—	—	4	134	363
1943	Husband	130	130	1	23	—	284	
	Wife	164	31	—	—	3	198	482
1944	Husband	112	135	1	35	3	286	
	Wife	155	42	2	—	2	201	487
1945	Husband	175	171	—	39	5	390	
	Wife	190	83	2	—	5	280	670
1946	Husband	251	257	4	56	3	571	
	Wife	249	100	1	—	3	353	924
1947	Husband	243	277	1	13	2	536	
	Wife	200	98	1	—	2	301	837
1948	Husband	136	100	—	6	1	243	
	Wife	153	52	—	—	—	205	448
1949	Husband	96	86	1	6	2	191	
	Wife	146	44	—	—	1	191	382
1950	Husband	114	57	—	9	1	181	
	Wife	106	49	—	—	—	155	336
1951	Husband	79	114	3	2	—	198	
	Wife	113	65	4	—	1	183	381
1952	Husband	105	120	—	2	1	228	
	Wife	104	61	2	—	1	168	396

GLOSSARY OF SOME LEGAL TERMS USED IN CONNECTION WITH NULLITY OF MARRIAGE

(1) *A Valid Marriage* is a marriage subject to no defect which might render it void or voidable.

(2) *A Void Marriage* is one subject to such defect as to fail in its primary intentions and legal effect (see Chapter III, p. 20 above).

(3) *A Voidable Marriage* is one subject to such defect as to be liable to fail in its primary intentions and legal effect if, but only if, one of the parties takes steps to "avoid" the marriage by appropriate action during their joint lives (see Chapter III, p. 22 above).

(4) *An Approbated Marriage* is a marriage, initially voidable, in which the party who would have been entitled to take appropriate legal action to "avoid" it has by his or her conduct become precluded from so doing. An example is where a marriage subject to the defect of sexual impotence has been approbated by the adoption of a child. The provisos to section 7 (1) of the Matrimonial Causes Act, 1937,[1] may be regarded as statutory approbation.

(5) *A Validated Marriage* is a marriage of doubtful validity (generally as to form) declared valid under the Provisional Order (Marriages) Act, 1905, or the Marriages Validity (Provisional Orders) Act, 1924, or by a special *ad hoc* Act of Parliament.

(6) *An Irregular Marriage* is one which fails to comply with the law so far as matters of form are concerned, but not so as to render it void (see Chapter III, p. 20). In former times a separate term, *clandestine marriage*, was used where the defect in form related to the publicity of marriage.

(7) *A Common Law Marriage* is marriage by exchange of consents, but without formalities. It is also called *Informal Marriage*, and in medieval and later documents the term "handfasting" is used as a synonym for it.[2] It was abrogated in the Roman Church by the Decree "*Tametsi*" of the Council of Trent, 1564; in the English Church by Canon 62 of 1603/4; in the English State by Lord Hardwicke's Act, 1753; and in Scotland only as recently as 1940 by the Marriage (Scotland) Act, 1939. It may still be contracted abroad in places where the English Common Law prevails and requirements of form cannot be complied with.

(8) *An Alleged Marriage* is a marriage asserted by some interested party, but denied or doubted by others. Formerly, alleged marriages were classified as follows: *ostensible; purported, pretended,* or *colourable; attempted; putative.* Since these distinctions are obsolete we have not thought it necessary to define them, but the curious may consult Burn's *Ecclesiastical Law,* Vol. II (1842 ed.).

---

1 Now Section 8 (1) of the Matrimonial Causes Act, 1950; see Appendix 1, p. 49 above.
2 For references to the use of the term "handfasting", see *The Oxford English Dictionary.*

MENTAL AFFLICTION AS RENDERING A MARRIAGE VOID OR VOIDABLE

MENTAL AFFLICTION varies in its incidence on the validity of the marriage. We think that it may be of assistance to attempt to review the various ways in which mental defect may invalidate a marriage.

(i) Such unsoundness of mind as vitiates consent renders the marriage void *ab initio*. In order to fall within this category there must be either such general unsoundness of mind as precludes the person in question from forming a rational judgement on any subject, or such delusions as affect the transaction of marriage into which he or she is entering. The marriage of a lunatic during a lucid interval will, therefore, be valid. Further, a party may have such delusions as to be quite insane: but if the delusions do not affect the transaction so as to vitiate true marital consent the marriage will be valid at Common Law. For example, a delusion that the party is being persecuted might well be insufficient to render invalid a marriage entered into by that party.

(ii) One of the methods of ascertaining whether a person was of such unsoundness of mind that he should be subjected to the various incapacities attaching to lunacy was to establish a commission to inquire into his mental state.[1] If it was thereby declared that he was of unsound mind he was known as a lunatic "so found by inquisition", or more shortly a lunatic "so found". As appears above[2] he was thereafter precluded from contracting a valid marriage: such a marriage was void *ab initio*. This amounted to a legal incapacity. It therefore differed from (i) above in that the party could not validly marry even during a lucid interval,[3] or even if he suffered from collateral delusions and was quite capable of understanding the nature of the marriage contract and the duties and responsibilities which it creates.

(iii) By the Matrimonial Causes Act, 1950, s. 8 (1) (b), the marriage is *voidable* at the suit of either party if either of them was at the time of the marriage of unsound mind or a mental defective within the meaning of the Mental Deficiency Acts.[4] This differs from (i) above in that the mental defect may not affect the capacity to understand the nature of the

---

[1] See Chapter III, p. 21.
[2] See Chapter III, p. 16.
[3] *Turner* v. *Meyers* (1808), 1 Hag. Con. 414, at p. 417.
[4] In the Mental Deficiency Act, 1927, s.1, mental defectives were classified as follows:

(a) Idiots, i.e., persons in whose case there exists mental defectiveness of such a degree that they are unable to guard themselves against common physical dangers;

(b) Imbeciles, i.e., persons in whose case there exists mental defectiveness which, though not amounting to idiocy, is yet so pronounced that they are incapable of managing themselves or their affairs . . .;

(c) Feeble-minded persons, i.e., persons in whose case there exists mental defectiveness which, though not amounting to imbecility, is yet so pronounced that they require care, supervision, and control for their own protection or for the protection of others . . .;

marriage contract or the responsibilities which it creates. It differs from (ii) above in that it applies whether or not there has been an inquisition of lunacy.

(iv) By a further provision of the Matrimonial Causes Act, 1950, s.8 (1) (b), the marriage is *voidable* at the suit of either party if either of them was at the time of the marriage subject to recurrent fits of insanity. This differs from (i) above, in that the mental defect need not affect the capacity to understand the nature of the marriage contract or the responsibilities which it creates. It differs from both (i) and (iii) above, in that the marriage is defeasible even though it takes place during a lucid interval. It differs from (ii) above, in that it applies whether or not there has been an inquisition of lunacy.

(d) Moral defectives, i.e., persons in whose case there exists mental defectiveness coupled with strongly vicious or criminal propensities, and who require care, supervision and control for the protection of others.

"Mental defectiveness" is defined as "a condition of arrested or incomplete development of mind existing before the age of 18 years, whether arising from inherent causes or induced by disease or injury."

APPENDIX 5

THE ROMAN CATHOLIC LAW OF NULLITY

Note: The list of grounds for nullity as recognized by Roman Canon Law, given below, has been checked through the kind offices of the Very Reverend Monsignor E. G. Dunderdale, L.J.C., Chancellor of the Roman Catholic Archdiocese of Westminster.

AS IS SHOWN in the Report of the Archbishops' Commission on Canon Law, 1947, the general Canon Law of the Western Church developed greatly between the fourth century and the sixteenth century when it was embodied in the compilation known as the *Corpus Juris Canonici*. Subject to certain changes of a minor nature, this was the law administered by the English Ecclesiastical Courts up to the time of the Reformation, and in the Roman Catholic Church up to the present time.

Grounds for Nullity of Marriage under the Canon Law were set out by Tancred in the thirteenth century as follows:

> Error, conditio, votum, cognatio, crimen,
> Cultus disparitas, vis, ordo, ligamen, honestas,
> Dissensus, et affinis, si clandestinus et impos,
> Raptave sit mulier, loco nec reddita tuto,
> Haec facienda vetant connubia, facta retractant.

These grounds were all *impedimenta dirimenta* forbidding marriage, but the lines do not include all the grounds contained in the *Corpus Juris*, as will be seen from the summary, set out below, of grounds of nullity under the Canon Law up to the Reformation:

(1) *Error de Persona*
Mistaken identity of other party to putative marriage.

Post-Reformation in England
Unchanged.

(2) *Error de conditione*
Marriage of a slave to a free person without the latter's knowledge of the former's status.

Already obsolete before Reformation.

(3) *Clandestinus*
Secret marriage ceremony lacking the prescribed ecclesiastical formalities; but up to the Council of Trent clandestine marriages were valid though illicit.

Not an impediment in England until Lord Hardwicke's Act, 1753.

(4) *Cognatio*
Consanguinity or blood relationship extending to even wider degrees than in the Levitical table. More remote degrees subject to Papal dispensation.

Limited by 25 H. 8, c. 22 and 32 H. 8, c. 38 (1533 and 1540) to table of kindred, Canon 99, 1603.

57

(5) *Affinis*

Relationship by marriage. In the case of illicit *copula* the prohibition did not extend to so many degrees.

Same as for Consanguinity (4) above.

(6) *Cognatio Spiritualis* (Canon 1079)

Marriage between minister and person he has baptized, or between sponsor and baptized person.

Not continued.

(7) *Cognatio Legalis*

Legal adoption (Canon 1080). Marriage barred between adopter and adopted.

Not continued, but now barred in certain circumstances by Adoption Act, 1949, ss. 11, 13.

(8) *Crimen*

Crime. Adultery of a spouse with paramour accompanied by promise to marry, or murder or attempted murder of other spouse; with result that guilty spouse and paramour can never intermarry.

Not continued.

(9) *Cultus disparitas*

Disparity of religion.

Not continued.

(10) *Vis et metus*

Fear, duress or constraint overbearing the will.

Unchanged.

(11) *Raptus*

Abduction. But, if willing, woman could marry captor even if in his power.

Unchanged; but really duress.

(12) *Ordo and Votum Sacer*

Holy Orders a bar to marriage. Vow of perfect and perpetual chastity on reception into subdiaconate.

Not continued. Marriage of the clergy expressly allowed by 2 & 3 Edw. 6, c. 21 (1548) and 5 & 6, Edw. 6, c. 12 (1552).

(13) *Ligamen*

Bond of existing marriage. Bigamy forbidden.

Unchanged, except by institution of divorce by Bill or judicial decree.

(14) *Publica Honestas*

(Connected with *Affinis*.) Offence against public decorum or decency, e.g., where party to marriage had repudiated solemn betrothal to a third person but marriage had not been consummated; or where party to a betrothal repudiated it and became betrothed to or espoused to a blood relation of other party in first degree.

Continued, though only with regard to pre-contracts of marriage, until Lord Hardwicke's Act, 1753.

(15) *Amentia*

Insanity at time of marriage.

Unchanged, covering mental incapacity.[1]

[1] See Appendix 4, p. 55, above.

(16) *Impotentia*
Impotence at time of marriage and continuing thereafter. Unchanged, but decree of Nullity only on plea of spouse.

(17) *Impedimentum Aetatis*
Non-age. Marriage null, subject to exceptional cases (*nisi malitia suppleat aetatem*), if male under 14 years or female under 12 years, unless confirmed by them after reaching stipulated ages.[1] Unchanged till Age of Marriage Act, 1929, see now Marriage Act, 1949, s. 2.[2]

(18) *Consensus*
Lack of consent or defective consent. (See Chapter IV of this Report.[3]) Not continued, except under categories (1), (10), and (15) above.

[1] Under the present Code the impediment lapses on completion of the sixteenth year for males and the fourteenth year for females.
[2] See Appendix 1, p. 49, above.
[3] See page 25 above.

APPENDIX 6

A LETTER FROM THE REGISTRAR-GENERAL CONCERNING CIVIL MARRIAGE CEREMONIES

Copy of letter from the General Register Office, Somerset House, London, W.C.2, to Noel Middleton, Esq., Q.C., dated 16 November 1950

SIR,

In reply to your letter of the 6th October I am directed by the Registrar-General to inform you that in November 1947 Superintendent Registrars in England and Wales were asked, at the civil marriage ceremony, to address the following words to the parties immediately before the recital of the declaratory and contracting words now prescribed by sections 45 (1) and 44 (3) of the Marriage Act, 1949. This was in the nature of a request rather than a mandatory instruction. So far as the Registrar-General is aware, it is likely to be generally observed.

"This place in which you are now met has been duly sanctioned according to law for the celebration of marriages.

"Before you are joined in matrimony it is my duty to remind you of the solemn and binding character of the vows you are about to make. Marriage according to the law of this country is the union of one man with one woman, voluntarily entered into for life, to the exclusion of all others."

The concluding sentence is now incorporated in the form of Notice of Marriage, and is also prominently displayed as a printed notice in every Register Office.

You are no doubt aware that the Denning Committee on Procedure in Matrimonial Causes interested themselves in this matter—vide paragraph 29 (xiii) of their Final Report (1947, Cmd. 7024).

I am, Sir,
Your obedient Servant,
(signed) J. M. ROSS

APPENDIX 7

THE NEW TESTAMENT TEACHING ON MARRIAGE AND DIVORCE

Memorandum prepared by
The Reverend Professor G. D. Kilpatrick, D.D.

THE FOLLOWING passages, Mark 10. 1–12; Luke 16. 18; Matt. 5. 31 f.; 19. 1–9; 1 Cor. 7. 10–16, are relevant to a discussion of the New Testament teaching on marriage and divorce. Before we compare their evidence we must first determine their text in a few particulars. Secondly, we have to examine the relationship of the passages in the Synoptic Gospels to try to establish which form of the tradition is most likely to be original and to account for the peculiar features of the sayings in Matthew. Thirdly, we shall relate the evidence of the Synoptic Gospels to 1 Cor. 7. In the fourth place one subsidiary point is treated.

Note: In the following discussion I use Souter's *Nouum Testamentum Graece* and indicate where another reading seems preferable or where the text is doubtful. I have discussed the passages in Matthew in my book, *The Origins of the Gospel According to St Matthew*, pp. 19, 29 f., 101–3. The present treatment is independent.

I. *The Synoptic Gospels: Text*

Mark 10, 1–12

(a) Verse 2, omit προσελθόντες Φαρισαῖοι.

In general, other things being equal, the shorter text is more likely to be right and here it is in keeping with Mark's style. The evangelist frequently uses the third person plural of verbs without any subject separately expressed. Scribes often added a subject, sometimes from another Gospel. Here the additional words may have been derived from Matt. 19. 3. This argument is derived from C. H. Turner, who stated it briefly in Gore's *New Commentary on Holy Scripture*, Vol. II, p. 86, where he commented on this verse. He gave the detailed evidence in the *Journal of Theological Studies*, Vol. XXV (1924), pp. 377–86, Vol. XXVI (1925), pp. 225–40, cf. Vol. XXIX (1927), p. 5. Turner was not concerned in his discussion with our problem. We shall see the relevance of the reading when we discuss the relation of this to the corresponding passage in Matthew.

(b) Verse 12, for ἀπολύσασα τὸν ἄνδρα αὐτῆς read ἐξέλθῃ ἀπὸ τοῦ ἀνδρὸς καί.

Most discussion of this verse has assumed the text in Souter's edition without noticing the alternative. Dr Charles, for example, apparently considered only the reading in Souter's text and argued that Mark is here unhistorical. According to him, "The law allowed no Jewish woman to divorce her husband."[1] There are two comments on this.

First, the reading preferred above would cover desertion or separation as well as divorce. It would be rash to assert that no Jewish woman ever left her husband. So with the change of text Mark is no longer open to Dr Charles' comment, even if his statement were true.

[1] See R. H. Charles, *The Teaching of the New Testament on Divorce*, pp. 27 ff., 85 ff.

This brings us to the second point. Dr Charles' statement is mistaken. No Jewish woman had an unrestricted right of divorce, but for certain prescribed grounds she could have the marriage dissolved.

This limited right of divorce goes back to the period of the schools of Shammai and Hillel, i.e., the first century A.D. A Jewish wife could have her marriage dissolved:

(a) if the illness or calling of her husband brought in its train certain nuisances which made the marriage intolerable (for example, leprosy or copper-smelting);

(b) if the husband compelled his wife to make promises, or made demands on her, which were demeaning or impossible;

(c) if a woman had been betrothed or given in marriage as a minor (i.e., under 12 years of age) after her father's death by her mother or her brothers, she could terminate the betrothal or marriage by a formal refusal. Against her father's disposition she had this right only if she had been divorced by her husband as a minor. In these divorces the wife had the right of remarriage.

The details will be found in Strack-Billerbeck, *Kommentar zum Neuen Testament aus Talmud und Midrasch*, Vol. I, pp. 318 f., Vol. II, pp. 23 f., Vol. IV, pp. 754 f.

The passage, Josephus, *Ant.* 15. 259, is ambiguous and can be translated somewhat as follows:

In the course of time it happened that Salome quarrelled with Costobarus and at once sent him a bill dissolving the marriage in a manner contrary to the laws of the Jews. For with us it is lawful for the husband to do this but not even a divorced woman who is on her own is allowed to marry unless her former husband permit.

All this need mean is that Jewish wives lacked the right of arbitrary divorce that their husbands had, not that they had no right of divorce at all.

Luke 16. 18

There are no problems of text or interpretation peculiar to this verse.

Matt. 5. 31 f.; 19. 1–9

There are few textual points in these verses.

(i) At 19. 9 some manuscripts read παρεκτὸς λόγου πορνείας instead of μὴ ἐπὶ πορνείᾳ. Probably the reading παρεκτὸς λόγου πορνείας at 19. 9 represents an attempt to assimilate this verse to 5. 32, where παρεκτὸς λόγου πορνείας occurs without variant. At 19. 9 one fifteenth-century manuscript, 1574, of Mount Athos, has according to von Soden neither μὴ ἐπὶ πορνείᾳ nor παρεκτὸς λόγου πορνείας. Tischendorf cites Tertullian and Athenagoras as having this omission. There is, however, nothing in their quotations to show that it is Matthew that they are quoting. I have not been able to find that any other witness has this omission. In these circumstances it seems probable that Matt. 19. 9 had μὴ ἐπὶ πορνείᾳ rather than παρεκτὸς λόγου πορνείας and most improbable that it had neither phrase.

(ii) At 19. 9 after μοιχᾶται many manuscripts add καὶ ὁ ἀπολελυμένην γαμήσας μοιχᾶται. This clause could easily have dropped out after the previous μοιχᾶται through homoeoteleuton (μοιχᾶται . . . μοιχᾶται).

(iii) At 5. 32 some manuscripts are without the clause καὶ ὃς ἐὰν ἀπολελυμένην γαμήσῃ μοιχᾶται. This variation corresponds to that in 19. 9 discussed just above. Homoeoteleuton may be responsible for the absence of the clause (μοιχευθῆναι . . . μοιχᾶται).

We may now summarize the results of our inquiry into the text of these passages:

(a) Mark 10. 2, omit προσελθόντες Φαρισαῖοι.

(b) Mark 10. 12, read ἐξέλθῃ ἀπὸ τοῦ ἀνδρὸς καὶ for ἀπολύσασα τὸν ἄνδρα αὐτῆς.

(c) Matt. 19. 9, keep μὴ ἐπὶ πορνείᾳ in the text.

(d) Matt. 19. 9 after μοιχᾶται add καὶ ὁ ἀπολελυμένην γαμήσας μοιχᾶται.

II. *The Synoptic Gospels: Literary Relationships*

We must discuss our passages in the light of our views on the relationships of the Synoptic Gospels as a whole. Theories about them are roughly of two kinds:

(i) The theories of fundamentalists who uphold the inerrancy of all Holy Scripture and are loath to describe any part of it as secondary to another part. They usually argue with various elaborations in detail that Matthew is the oldest Gospel.

(ii) The theory about the relationships of the Synoptic Gospels held by many scholars, apart from the fundamentalists, that Mark is the oldest Gospel, that Matthew and Luke both used Mark and used in addition a second source called Q. Furthermore, for their peculiar discourse material Matthew and Luke each probably used another source (M, L). I shall discuss our passage in the light of this theory.

(1) *The Relationship of Mark 10. 1–12 and Matt. 19. 1–9*

On this theory Matthew will depend on Mark, and we shall explain any differences between the two as editorial revision of Mark by Matthew or as due to the use of another source by Matthew. If we read, as I have suggested, the longer text at the end of Matt. 19. 9, we have one agreement between Matthew and Luke which we may ascribe to the use of Q.

There are difficulties in this treatment of the relationship of the two passages, as was indicated by Canon B. H. Streeter in *The Four Gospels*, p. 259. Matthew is "more closely related to Jewish usage than the parallel in Mark (Mark 10. 2–12)". This is true not merely for this passage but also for other passages where Mark and Matthew are parallel. Matthew seems the more Jewish of the two and so, it is argued, the more original. Consequently we must throw over the results of the labours of many scholars on the Synoptic problem and in this and similar instances follow Matthew as being more reliable than Mark.

Not merely is this argument drastic. It is also mistaken; and the mistake lies in our taking in an uncritical way the evidence of certain sources as the norm of Judaism in our Lord's time. It is as though we were to take accounts of the restored French monarchy of 1815 as reliable evidence for France before 1789. Even though the monarchists of 1815 were anxious to put back the clock, great differences in circumstances and outlook made anything like a real restoration impossible, and pictures of France from 1815 and later were quite inapplicable to the eighteenth century. In the same way Rabbinic Judaism of after A.D. 70 has a number of statements about Judaism which are often taken as the norm for all accounts or statements relating to the earlier period.

After A.D. 70 the Pharisee Johanan ben Zacchai and his followers and supporters set about reconstructing Judaism on the Pharisaic pattern as they saw it. Their two principles in this reconstruction were uniformity and conformity. They had to start by bringing about uniformity in the teaching of Pharisaism or Rabbinic Judaism itself, a process that seems to have taken place in A.D. 70–90. It is in this connection that we hear so much about the various Pharisaic schools, especially about the differences between the disciples of Hillel and those of Shammai, and it is in this period that decisions were made between the views of the schools, including decisions on the grounds for which a man could divorce his wife. We have seen that the ruling that in certain conditions a wife could have her marriage dissolved goes back to this period.

If this picture is reliable the Judaism to which Matthew is "more closely related" is the Rabbinic Judaism of after A.D. 70, and this very resemblance is a ground for treating Matthew, not as the more original, but as the later and historically secondary account.

Let us see how this applies to Mark 10. 1–12 and Matt. 19. 1–9. In Mark there is probably no reference to Pharisees or Rabbinic leaders and the issue is a general one: can a man divorce his wife? Matthew differs from Mark in the following three particulars among others:

(1) verse 3, the addition of a reference to the Pharisees;
(2) verse 3, the addition of κατὰ πᾶσαν αἰτίαν;
(3) verse 9, the addition of μὴ ἐπὶ πορνείᾳ.

These changes bring the story into line with the features of A.D. 70–90. In these years the issue between Hillelites and Shammaites which the Rabbinic leaders had to solve was not whether a man could divorce his wife, but what were the grounds on which he could do so. The school of Shammai argued that a man could divorce his wife only for unchastity. The school of Hillel held that he could do so for almost any reason. The issue was decided in favour of the school of Hillel. We can now see how the form of the story in Matthew fits in with these conditions as the Marcan form does not.

If we accept this interpretation, it becomes unnecessary to jettison so much scholarly work on the Synoptic problem. On the other hand, it follows that in comparison with Mark Matthew is entirely secondary from the historical point of view. If we want to find out what our Lord said we have to start from Mark, not Matthew.

In support of this conclusion there is one piece of evidence in Matthew which W. C. Allen pointed out. Unless Matt. 19. 10 f. is an argument for an incredible laxity, we must conclude that the ruling that the disciples considered so hard is not that of Matt. 19. 9 but that of Mark 10. 11 f. This is another indication of Matthew's dependence on Mark.

(2) *Luke 16. 18 and Matt. 5. 32; 19. 9*

We can see from the synopses that Matt. 5. 32 and 19. 9 have agreements with Luke 16. 18 against Mark 10. 11. The agreements cover nearly all the wording of Luke 16. 18. From these facts we may infer that at this point Matthew and Luke are using Q, as Luke differs more from Mark. Luke follows the wording of Q closely.

We may summarize our conclusions as follows. Mark 10. 2–12 is a primary source. For the tradition contained in Mark 10. 2–9 we are entirely dependent on Mark. Mark 10. 10 ff. is parallel to Q, Matt. 5. 32/Luke 16. 18, where the saying seems to have circulated independently of any context. This difference in tradition between Mark 10. 2–9 and 10. 10–12, verses 10–12 being parallel to Q, corresponds to the fact that in Mark there is a real break between 10. 9 and 10. 10–12. We may conjecture that the new setting in Mark 10. 10 is provided by the evangelist, but the important thing to realize is that the second saying has been handed down in the Synoptic Gospels in two traditions, that of Mark 10. 11 f. and that of Luke 16. 18/Matt. 5. 32. As we shall see from 1 Cor. 7, St Paul probably knew this saying in a form somewhat like that of Mark. If these conclusions are sound, the passage must be old indeed and can scarcely have better credentials. If the saying does not come from Jesus, it must have entered the Christian tradition in the years immediately after his death, when the number of first-hand witnesses of what Jesus said and did was at its greatest. One difficulty alleged against the form of the saying in Mark is that it provides for divorce by the wife, a form of divorce not recognized by Jewish law. We have discussed this difficulty above and have suggested reasons for discounting it. We must, however, recognize that Rawlinson, *St Mark*, p. 135, and W. Knox, *The Sources of the Synoptic Gospels*, Vol. I, p. 69, regard 10. 10–12 as secondary. Vincent Taylor, *St Mark*, pp. 419 ff., is more cautious and would adopt the same reading in Mark 10. 12 as is suggested in this memorandum.

(3) *The Modification of Matt. 5. 32; 19. 9*

We can scarcely account for this modification by appealing to the difference between *Halakah* and *Haggadah*. The Beatitudes are *Haggadah*, edification. On the other hand, Mark 10. 11 f., Luke 16. 18, Matt. 5. 31–7 seem to be examples of *Halakah*, rules governing conduct. We must remember that even John 15. 12, "that ye love one another", is described as ἐντολή, though we would regard "love one another" as a general principle rather than as law.

An explanation of how such modifications arose can, however, be drawn from the nature of *Halakah*. If by *Halakah* we understand the body of Jewish Law as determining conduct, we must recognize that it displayed a flexibility that is not always realized. For example, the law of the Sabbath was modified to permit of self-defence in war on the Sabbath (1 Macc. 2. 29–41), even though the law of the Sabbath was divinely given at Sinai. Again, according to Deut. 15. 1–3, all loans were cancelled at the beginning of every seventh year. This provision made it impossible to obtain credit in the fifth or sixth year. Hillel introduced a device, the *prosbul*, which got round the provisions of Deut. 15. 1–3 and enabled the creditor to retain his rights despite the Torah. Other examples and a discussion will be found in Moore, *Judaism*, Vol. I, part I, chapter III, "The Unwritten Law". From this evidence it becomes clear that the law was not treated as a rigid and inflexible code that could not be modified. Where it had become intolerable it was relaxed by explicit amendment or legal fiction or reinterpretation.

We may go on to argue that where a case was made out a similar flexibility would be practised in Christian communities under the influence of Jewish tradition. Even if they felt that they were dealing with divine Law, Christians might have no qualms in adjusting the teaching of Jesus to the circumstances, as Israel had adjusted the Law of Moses.

We may have an example of such modification in 1. Cor. 7. 11a, 15. It was clear that a union of a Christian and a pagan might become intolerable and so, if the pagan partner wished to dissolve the marriage, it was to be dissolved. There was no call to tolerate the intolerable.

The rule about almsgiving provides another instance of modification. The Gospel said "Give to him that asketh thee" (Matt. 5. 42). Already the abuses suggested by such a command are causing difficulty in the Didache 1. 6 and the commandment itself is modified in Clement of Alexandria (GCS. iii. 225): "We must give alms, but with discrimination, and to the worthy only."

III. *The Synoptic Gospels and 1 Cor. 7. 10f.*

We have suggested that we depend on Mark 10. 2–12 and Luke 16. 18 for our knowledge of what Jesus said about divorce, where Mark 10. 11 f. is parallel to Luke 16. 18. In order to determine the relation of these passages we must refer also to 1 Cor. 7. 10f.

1 Cor. 7. 10f. refers to a saying of Jesus, τοῖς δὲ γεγαμηκόσιν παραγγέλλω οὐκ ἐγὼ

6

ἀλλὰ ὁ κύριος, and contains two parts, γυναῖκα ἀπὸ ἀνδρὸς μὴ χωρισθῆναι and ἄνδρα γυναῖκα μὴ ἀφιέναι.

Here χωρισθῆναι is a normal term for the divorce of married couples, for example, in the papyrus, PSI 166, ἀπ᾽ ἀλλήλων χωρισθῆναι.

In containing two parts, one referring to the woman and the other to the man, 1 Cor. 7. 10f. resembles Mark 10. 11f., which likewise contains two parts referring severally to the man and the woman. To this extent 1 Corinthians agrees with Mark against Luke 16. 18 where both clauses refer to the man. On the other hand, in this saying Mark and Luke agree against 1 Cor. 7. 10f. in treating of remarriage after divorce and not of divorce itself. Thus Mark stands between Luke and St Paul. In this connection it looks as though St Paul had recast something like Mark 10. 11f. in the light of Mark 10. 9. Thus our argument favours the view that we find the original form of the saying of Jesus in Mark 10. 11f. as against Luke 16. 18.

There is another consideration which points in the same direction. Luke 16. 18 discusses divorce from the point of the man: can he marry again after divorce? and can he marry a divorced woman? Matt. 19 agrees with Luke in this and further authorizes the man to divorce his wife for unchastity, but says nothing about her divorcing him for any reason. The nearest we come to any consideration of the woman is at Matt. 5. 32 ποιεῖ αὐτὴν μοιχευθῆναι.

In St Paul we find both tendencies: one to treat woman as subordinate to man, e.g., at 1 Cor. 11. 3–16; 14. 33–6; and the other to treat the sexes as on an equality, as at 1 Cor. 7. 1–16. There is no need to ask whence St Paul derived his teaching in which woman was subordinate: it was too widespread a point of view at the time. On the other hand, teaching which put woman on an equality with man was less common, and it seems at least possible that St Paul had arrived at it by meditating on some such sayings of our Lord as those of Mark, 10. 1–12. Further, Matthew and Luke, with their insistence on the masculine point of view, both represent to that extent a declension from the teaching of Jesus.

Our argument thus leads to the conclusion that our Lord's teaching is more reliably represented by Mark 10. 1–12. This conclusion arises out of a comparison of this passage with those in the other Synoptic Gospels and with 1 Cor. 7. 10f. To treat Mark as secondary would be to turn our backs on much scholarly work on our documents, and we have found it unnecessary to do this. Where Mark and Q parted company we saw that Mark had the support of St Paul. This fact led to the opinion that Mark gave us our primary account, a view that was supported by the consideration that Mark's account provided a much less one-sided picture of the relation of the sexes than the accounts of Matthew and Luke did. This last point is an important one and in our concern with the problem we often lose sight of it.

IV. *Subsidiary Point*

πορνεία. If we insist on the strict meaning of this word we must translate it by "prostitution". If that is so, Matt. 5, 19 will mean not that a man may divorce his wife for adultery in general, but only for one extreme and repeated kind of adultery. The passages will be quite consistent and intelligible on this interpretation.

On the other hand, the following interpretation is commoner. πορνεία can mean unchastity in general, and, in this kind of context, adultery. For example, at Ecclus. 23. 23 we have the expression ἐν πορνείᾳ ἐμοιχεύθη used of the woman. This interpretation harmonizes with the evidence of the Jewish sources. λόγος πορνείας can translate the phrase דְּבַר עֶרְוָה used in this connection at M. Gittin 9. 10 and deriving from עֶרְוַת דָּבָר Deut. 24. 1. This also will give a coherent meaning to our passages.

THE GOSPEL PASSAGES DEALING WITH THE DISSOLUTION OF MARRIAGE

Memorandum prepared by
the late the Reverend R. G. Heard, M.B.E., M.C., M.A.,
Fellow of Peterhouse and University Lecturer in Divinity, Cambridge[1]

TWO MAJOR points appear to be at issue: (*a*) the meaning of *porneia* in Matt.5. 32; 19. 9; and (*b*) the relative authority of Matt. 5. 31-2; 19. 9; Mark 10, 11-12; and Luke 16. 18 as expressing the teaching of our Lord.

Porneia

1. The normal meaning of the word is "unchastity"—in a general sense, cf. in the N.T., e.g., Col. 3. 5, Rev. 9. 21.

2. This meaning is sometimes made more specific from the context, e.g., 1 Cor. 5. 1, where the "fornication" consists of "having his father's wife", Jude 7, where the allusion appears to be sodomy, and a number of places where "fornication" serves as a good translation. (Cf. also the figurative use of *porneia* for idolatry in the LXX.)

3. The interpretation of *porneia* in the special sense of "unchastity between betrothal and marriage" (as by Selwyn in *Theology*, 1927, p. 98) does not rest on any established use of *porneia* elsewhere in this sense, but on the assumption that "Matthew" was writing for readers who would so interpret it.

4. Opinion is divided as to whether *porneia* in the decree of the Council of Jerusalem (Acts 15) means "unchastity" in general or specifically "marriage within the degrees prohibited in Lev. 26. 6-26". The evidence adduced for this latter view depends entirely on the interpretation of certain N.T. passages, and is not supported—as far as I know—by the citation of any Greek passage outside the N.T. where a similar use of *porneia* can be demonstrated.

5. While *porneia* is sometimes found as a description of adulterous conduct, there appears to be normally in such passages an additional element of unchastity—e.g., harlotry, Amos 7. 17 (LXX); promiscuity, Hos. 2. 4-7 (LXX); a sin committed by both married and unmarried men, 1 Cor. 10. 8 (cf. Num. 25. 9); continuance in adultery, Hermas, *Man.* 4. 1, 5—and *porneia* seems always to be distinguished in some way from the more technical *moicheia*.

6. The following meanings for *porneia* in Matt. 5. 32; 19. 9 are possible, but while each of them has the support of good scholars, they are not to be regarded as equally likely. I have put them in an order corresponding to their nearness to the general usage of *porneia* outside the N.T.:

(1) Unchastity (in a general sense)
(2) "Aggravated" adultery, e.g., repeated, harlotry, etc.
(3) Simple adultery
(4) Unchastity between betrothal and marriage
(5) Relationship within the prohibited degrees

[1] This memorandum had not been corrected for publication by the Rev. R. G. Heard before his death.

The Relative Authority of Matt. 5. 31–2; 19. 3–9; Mark 10. 11–12, and Luke 16. 18
as expressing the Teaching of Our Lord

1. Most scholars would accept Luke 16. 18 as (a) a Q passage of which Matt. 5. 32 is a variant parallel, (b) a generally faithful reproduction of Q (as opposed to Matt. 5. 32), (c) a faithful reproduction of the sense of a saying of our Lord. The saying brands as adultery the marriage of a man to another woman after divorcing his wife, or the marriage of a man to a divorced woman. This injunction fits the Palestinian conditions of our Lord's time when normally only the man was able to initiate divorce. (Billerbeck has collected rabbinic evidence for a woman being permitted to divorce her husband (a) when certain types of illness contracted by her husband, or certain types of calling (e.g., copper-smelting, tanning) followed by her husband made the continuation of the marriage intolerable, (b) when her husband made her vow to carry out unworthy or impossible conditions, (c) when the wife had been betrothed as a minor (under 12 years of age) after her father's death by her mother or brothers (or even if she had been betrothed by her father in a case where she had already been divorced as a minor).)

2. Mark 10. 11 is generally accepted as giving the sense of a genuine saying of Jesus. It adds to Luke 16. 18a that the adultery is "against his wife".

3. Mark 10. 12, which assumes the possibility of a wife divorcing her husband, is against the Jewish Law (but see above), and perhaps a majority of scholars to-day would hesitate to accept this verse as actually spoken by Jesus. Many scholars would certainly regard it as a "legitimate" extension of Jesus' words in early Christian tradition to suit conditions in Gentile communities; Dr T. W. Manson regards it as a misunderstanding of the Aramaic which underlies Luke 16. 18b.

4. Most scholars regard Matt. 19. 3–9 as based on Mark 10. 1–12 with editorial modifications by "Matthew". A very large majority would consider these modifications as not due to a more precise knowledge of the actual incident but as made by "Matthew" (a) from his knowledge of Jewish custom in the addition of "for every cause" (19. 3) and the omission of Mark 10. 12 (b) from the tradition or practice of his community in the alteration of Mark 10. 11 by the addition of "the exceptive clause". The omission of "against her" after "committeth adultery" is interpreted by some scholars as due to the influence of the Q form (Matt. 5. 32; Luke 16. 18) on "Matthew's" wording here.

5. Matt. 5. 31–2 is widely accepted as a Q passage modified by "Matthew". There are, of course, many views as to the composition of "Matthew's" Sermon on the Mount; some scholars hold that the form of Matt. 5. 31–2 suggests an insertion by "Matthew" into the general series of our Lord's new commandments on Murder, Adultery, Swearing, Retaliation, Love of Neighbour, which "Matthew" may have drawn in the main from some other written source. Certainly 5. 31–2 as a whole, and especially "the exceptive clause", do not fit in well with the general stress on "motive" in the preceding paragraph. The majority view is that "Matthew" in 5. 31–2 has modified a Q saying by the addition of "the exceptive clause", and that this clause is drawn by "Matthew" from the tradition or practice of his community. The further alteration "maketh her to commit adultery" in place of "and marrieth another, committeth adultery" (Luke 16. 18) is generally taken as also editorial, and as implying that if the woman marries again she becomes an adulteress.

There are, in this case, two possibilities. *Either* a practice adopted because of the hardness of our Lord's teaching has been later given his authority, whether by "Matthew" or by a previously existing tradition (the view of the great majority of scholars), *or* the tradition goes back to our Lord's teaching. This raises in turn the meaning of *porneia* here and in 19. 9; on the usual interpretation of *porneia* there is a clear inconsistency between "Matthew's" teaching and that of Luke 16. 18 and Mark 10. 11, which are generally accepted as the teaching of our Lord.

6. St Paul's teaching, as from the Lord, in 1 Cor. 7. 10–11 is in close agreement with that of Mark 10. 11–12. Opinion is divided as to whether 10–11a, like Mark 10. 12, are to be taken as dependent on a saying of our Lord directly forbidding the woman also to divorce her husband and remarry, or as a "legitimate" extension of our Lord's teaching.

Note: In general, Appendix IV of the Report on *The Church and Marriage* still gives a good summary of the most widely held views of New Testament scholars to-day. Question 3, "Do the words *parektos logou porneias* belong to the original teaching of our Lord?", was answered then and would be answered now with an "almost unanimous" NO.

AN ANTHROPOLOGICAL AND BIOLOGICAL ANALYSIS OF THE NATURE, PLACE, AND FUNCTION OF MONO-GAMY IN THE INSTITUTION OF MARRIAGE

by Professor E. O. James, D.LITT., D.D., PH.D., F.S.A.

Marriage and the Natural Law

THE ORIGINS of marriage, like the beginnings of other social institutions, in the nature of the available evidence are largely conjectural and inductive. Nevertheless, there are biological, anthropological, sociological, and psychological reasons for assuming that some form of marriage is an aspect of the natural law for the human species since it is an essential requirement of its peculiar and unique status, constitution, and circumstances in the evolutionary process. Although apparently neither man nor the primates nearest to him (e.g., the anthropoids) lived gregariously in herds and packs, from their first appearance on the earth human beings seem to have been compelled to live in association with one another in order to survive and to give expression to their essential nature—i.e., to the endowments and attributes that constitute personality. Moreover, mating ceased to be an instinctive sporadic act of propagation isolated from its consequences in domesticity because, as in the case of the anthropoids, the offspring required prolonged maternal care and paternal protection by reason of their inability to fend for themselves immediately after birth. At the human level the infancy period of helplessness became extended so that before one child was self-sustaining in the ordinary course of events another would have been born of the same parents, since they were compelled to cohabit to maintain the offspring they had already produced. The subsequent births prolonged cohabitation until it became a permanent association—the father providing the food and shelter, the mother attending to the domestic needs of the growing family and the household. Consequently, mating under these conditions ceased to be a temporary liaison and the family, consisting of father, mother, and their children, became the nucleus of society in which the instincts, impulses, sentiments, and emotions involved in home-making and home life found their natural expression.

Brought together in this intimate manner, a psycho-social relationship was established between members of the same homestead which went much deeper than a voluntary co-operative group-consciousness for purely practical purposes of survival, protection, and economic advantage. The instincts which enable ants, bees, fishes, and mammals to pursue a static co-operative existence by subordinating the individual to the welfare of the group, in man acquired a dynamic character. To protection, propagation, and sustenance were added mutual assistance, personal friendship, and love, fellowship, and sympathy, by virtue of his higher mental endowments and attributes as a rational being. Within the nucleolus, or core, of this social unit (i.e., the family) the closest of human ties in the psycho-physical nuptial relationship of husband and wife has arisen in which man and woman constitute two parts of a complete whole, the one complementary to the other.

Each possesses independent qualities capable of being resolved into a personal unity in a permanent symbiosis absent in other species.

Thus, animals may live in a close association, and as members of a pack display a keenly developed community spirit, but they lack the ability to establish *personal* relationships because, while they have an instinctive awareness of other species of their own natural order and are subject to sex attraction, they are devoid of a rational consciousness to enable them to reflect upon their common nature, and its attributes, or to display such personal qualities and sentiments as love, sympathy, loyalty, respect, duty, and obedience.[1] In man gregariousness has passed into society with the individual subordinate to, but an integral part of, the social group and of the family, rooted and grounded in the nuptial relationship.

The primary division of this inter-personal relationship in which the group-maintaining instincts find their centre is the union of husband and wife for the purpose of creating the family, so that the twain became one in parenthood and home-making, and in the fulfilment of their respective personalities as a unified whole. Therefore, at the centre of the domestic nucleus lies the institution of marriage, and from it a wider sequence of relationships has emerged in the organization of laws of kinship, partly as a result of natural descent, and partly as a means of regulating sexual intercourse and other intimate associations between members of the same family and household and their respective relatives.

The Origin and Development of Monogamy

That the original constitution of human society was composed of very small groups consisting of perhaps a single male and female and their offspring, living and roaming about together as separate and independent entities, is suggested by the archaeological evidence. Thus, the remains of very small habitations on the lower slopes of hills, at the foot of steep cliffs, and on the banks of rivers, especially in places where nodules of flint and pebbles were at hand for the manufacture of implements, occur in interglacial Palaeolithic deposits, when the climate was sufficiently mild to render life in the open possible. When the temperature fell rapidly during glaciations, the shelter of caves was sought. The discovery of ashes in the cave deposits at Chou Kou Tien near Peking shows that fire-making was known very early in the Pleistocene Period, and it came into general use in inhabited caves in Europe during the later glaciations as the means of protection against the inclemency of the weather and the attacks of wandering and ravening beasts (bears, wolves, etc.). Under these more strenuous conditions family and social life appear to have developed around the domestic hearth. Living together at close quarters in small isolated family groups, if home life was to be harmonious and free from disturbing sexual rivalries and jealousies, domestic relations had to be maintained and organized in an orderly manner. Therefore, in all probability, it was within this context of the closely knit family group that the law of incest and the widespread practice of exogamy were established to prevent inbreeding, competitive courtships, and unregulated unions between amorous unattached males and no less responsive females.

Thus, when we turn to the anthropological data it becomes clear that the normal mode of life among peoples in a primitive state of culture, living under conditions almost indistinguishable from those that prevailed in Palaeolithic times (i.e., food-gatherers and lower hunters as distinct from agriculturists and herders), is the monogamous family

1 It may be true that in animals under the purely artificial conditions of domestication some of these qualities may be discerned in a nascent form, but this is due to the human environment and does not occur in the natural state.

hedged round with an elaborate system of tabus, and a social organization regulating inter-marriage between individuals and groups, directed in particular to the prevention of sexual relations with near relatives. Incest, in fact, is the sin *par excellence* in primitive society. Outside the family group, in which "prohibited degrees" are strictly enforced (often on pain of death) casual and temporary liaisons, it is true, are condoned, provided they do not infringe the law of incest or upset the harmony of the group. Extraneous alliances of this nature, however, stand on quite a different level from lawful marriage as the nucleus of organized family life. Such casual matings may be a carry-over from sub-human instinctive propagation, whereas the nuptial union is an institution peculiar to humanity and operative within the carefully guarded *milieu* of the home. Mating is individualistic in tendency; marriage is social and personal in its form, implications, and regulation. Sexual communism is, and apparently always has been, incompatible with social cohesion and the essential nature of man, as the U.S.S.R. has now discovered.

Among peoples in a very primitive state of culture (the Lower food-gatherers, such as the Veddas of Ceylon, the pre-Dravidians of Southern India, the Andamanese, the Pygmies, and the Fuegians of South America) monogamy is almost universal, except in the case of the Australian aborigines (which will be considered later) and the South African Bushmen. This may be explained perhaps partly on account of the relative equality in the number of males and females and the restrictive economic conditions (comparable to those that existed in the Palaeolithic), causing small groups consisting of a single family of several generations to wander about in search of the means of subsistence. In the Malay Peninsula the Semang, like the Veddas, are normally monogamous and infidelity is punished by death. After the birth of a child the parents very seldom separate, though occasionally additional wives may be taken, if the consent of all concerned is given. Despite a good deal of pre-nuptial licence, once marriage has been contracted and, as it were, ratified in the firstborn, conjugal infidelity and divorce were rare in the Andaman Islands before a penal settlement was established. The Pygmies seldom have more than one wife, even though they may consort with women from neighbouring tribes from time to time. On the whole, however, they are chaste.

Turning to the native tribes of Australia, which belong to the same cultural level,[1] we are confronted with a much more complex matrimonial organization than among these other very simple food-gathering communities. Malinowski has described no less than forty-nine methods of obtaining wives in this area (*The Family among the Australian Aborigines*, 1913, pp. 34ff.), but in every case the woman must belong to the right division of the tribe, the right locality, and the right age-group. Even where so-called "group marriage" is permitted (i.e., among the Dieri and Urabunna tribes) the primary union, known as *tippa-malku*, is an individual permanent marriage between one man and one woman. This, however, is supplemented by an extension of marital rights to a sort of "group-wife", or *pirrauru*, with whom a man is allowed to consort when he is temporarily separated from his proper partner (i.e., his *tippa-malku* wife). But the *pirrauru* must stand in the relation of "spouseship" (*noa*) to the particular group of men with whom she is permitted to have sexual intercourse under these conditions. Therefore, in theory the practice is a kind of legalized form of wedlock permitting conjugal rights under carefully guarded conditions among certain members of a joint domestic group, carrying with it mutual rights, duties,

[1] The Australian aborigines are a "Stone Age people," in the sense that they have no knowledge of the cultivation of crops or, except for the dog, of the domestication of animals. For tools they rely entirely on stone, chert, etc.

and responsibilities. (The evidence is set out in detail by A. W. Howitt, *Native Tribes of South-east Australia*, 1904, pp. 175 ff.) The *pirrauru* is neither a concubine nor a mistress, and since before she can occupy this position in the nuptial group she must be *tippa-malku* to one man exclusively, the deviation does not really alter the fact that monogamy of a loose kind is regarded as the normal form of marriage,[1] though in some of the Australian tribes, apart from this specialized system of "group marriage", polygyny is permitted. This is also the case among the Bushmen of South Africa (another Stone Age people). But taking the Lower hunters and food-gatherers collectively, monogamy is the general rule, either exclusively or with extraneous alliances outside the family organization and the law of incest in the form of casual alliances or temporary spouses. In the Higher hunters, especially in North America, polygyny is more frequent, but in the transitional phase between the food-gathering and food-production stage of cultural development (i.e., when hunting and collecting are combined with hoe agriculture and simple domestication of animals), when the wife is responsible for the "garden" and the hoeing of the fields near the settlement, while the husband with his sons is engaged in the chase, monogamy is very prevalent.

Polygamy

It is not until agriculture and/or herding have become fully established as the main or sole source of subsistence that *polygyny* (i.e., the marriage of one man with several women) has been widely adopted. With the development of husbandry on the grand scale, the incorporation of additional wives to increase the offspring and to meet the growing demands of the farm has become a valuable asset rather than a liability. A multiplicity of productive workers and potential mothers lessens the labours of all and brings more grist to the mill. Thus, in this type of society in Africa, for instance, monogamy is rare even among commoners, while chiefs and the ruling class often have maintained vast establishments of wives and concubines. In Ashanti the law is said to have limited the king to 3,333 wives; in Uganda the king of Loango was alleged to have had 7,000 wives, and different writers have estimated the female retinue of the king of Benin at anything from 600 to 4,000! These numbers may have been exaggerated, but royal households in these regions have been quite enormous. At this stage in the development of polygyny the usefulness of wives, though still in some measure a factor in the case, is quite secondary to the prestige acquired by a great harem as a sign of wealth (cf. 1 Kings 11. 3; Song of Songs 6. 8). In pastoral society, where monogamy has been very rare indeed, the same principles apply, the number of wives increasing with the prosperity of the herder. Nevertheless, the unique position occupied by the "chief wife" in a polygynous household suggests that even in these artificial conditions there is an underlying monogamous foundation of the family unit. Moreover, each wife usually has her own hut and separate household.

The marriage of several men to one woman (*polyandry*) is only of sporadic occurrence, found mainly in Tibet and India, and is occasioned by the paucity of women and adverse economic conditions compelling brothers to live together and share a single wife. But here again it is modified in a monogamous direction by the first brother to be married usually

---

1 In this connection it may be recalled that notwithstanding the monogamus tradition of Christendom, concubinage and even polygyny were condoned in isolated instances, and the latter practice was revived among the Anabaptists during the Reformation period. Moreover, wife lending and wife exchange have been by no means unknown under modern conditions, notably in the slums of great cities. In primitive society, at least, these abuses were regulated in the interests of the integrity of the family unit.

assuming the position of the "chief husband". The rest are regarded more in the nature of recognized paramours during the absence of the husband-in-chief, who sometimes "fathers" all the children born in the household.

Therefore, taking the evidence collectively, it would seem that monogamy is the normal form of marriage because it satisfies most adequately the natural law governing the nature of man and the constitution of the family as the nucleus of society. Polygamous deviations, either in the form of polygyny or polyandry, have arisen out of artificial conditions created chiefly by social and economic development associated with agriculture and herding. Apart from the practical advantages that have accrued from these practices and the particular circumstances in which they have arisen, a taste for sexual variety and novelty, especially on the part of the male, in some measure may have been responsible for polygyny and extra-marital liaisons. Nevertheless, the form of *marriage* that has been universally adopted and generally approved has been monogamy, because it alone meets the fundamental requirements of human personality and of society rooted in the family.

The Duration of Marriage

As regards the stability of marriage, the union normally has been contracted for life, although while divorce is said to be unknown among some food-gathering and hunting tribes and a few primitive agriculturists, usually it has been a frequent occurrence in primitive states of culture and in the ancient civilizations, particularly in the case of adultery on the part of the wife and in that of her barrenness. Desertion or ill-treatment and neglect by the husband also have been grounds for dissolution, and sometimes more trivial causes, e.g., refusal to mend clothes, burning food in cooking, etc.

In ancient Greece and Rome, as in Vedic India, monogamy was rigidly maintained as a union of great stability, until in Periclean Athens divorce became as easily obtainable as it was subsequently in Ciceronian Rome—at any rate among the ruling classes. Of Ancient Egypt singularly little is known on this subject, but although it seems that a man could take more than one legitimate wife, and keep numerous concubines, few appear to have availed themselves of the opportunity. In the tomb-paintings the wife is always shown accompanying her husband, whether he be feasting or hunting, and she is often referred to on the wall-inscriptions as "his beloved", or "his darling". That the union was permanent is indicated by the counsel of Ptah-hotep in his book of wise sayings: "Love thy wife at home, as it beseemeth. Fill her belly, clothe her back; unguent is the remedy for her limbs. Gladden her heart, so long as she liveth; she is a goodly field for her lord." In China a husband could divorce his wife not only for barrenness but also for disregard of his parents, talkativeness, and ill temper, but she was not allowed to desert her husband for any cause. Similarly, in the Semitic cultures a man was free to repudiate his spouse at will. Among the Jews, however, this unlimited right gradually ceased and eventually was abolished. But although a man then had to produce adequate grounds for a dissolution, a woman had and has no reciprocal rights. In Islamic law all that is required to annul a marriage is for a man to pronounce thrice the formula, "I divorce thee", though an interval of four months must elapse before the decree is made absolute. The polygynous pastoral tradition so deeply laid in the Qur'an, the frequency of divorce, and the absence of any sacramental significance attached to the nuptial bond, have rendered family life in Islam notoriously unstable. But, as in the case of the Jews, when living in a predominantly monogamous society Moslems seldom have had more than one wife.

TABLE OF STATUTES

TABLE OF CASES

INDEX